SHAKEDOWN CRUISE

BY THE SAME AUTHOR

Boatowner's Mechanical and Electrical Manual (4th edition, McGraw Hill/
   Adlard Coles)
Marine Diesel Engines (3rd edition, McGraw Hill/Adlard Coles)
Nigel Calder's Cruising Handbook (McGraw Hill)
How to Read a Nautical Chart (2nd edition, McGraw Hill)
Cuba: A Cruising Guide (Imray)

SHAKEDOWN CRUISE

CRUISE

LESSONS AND ADVENTURES FROM A CRUISING VETERAN AS HE LEARNS THE ROPES

Nigel Calder

ADLARD
COLES

LONDON · OXFORD · NEW YORK · NEW DELHI · SYDNEY

ADLARD COLES
Bloomsbury Publishing Plc

50 Bedford Square, London, WC1B 3DP, UK

www.adlardcoles.com

BLOOMSBURY, ADLARD COLES and the Adlard Coles logo are trademarks of Bloomsbury
Publishing Plc

First published in Great Britain 2018

A catalogue record for this book is available from the British Library

Library of Congress Cataloguing-in-Publication data has been applied for

ISBN: HB: 978-1-4729-4671-3
eBook: 978-1-4729-4668-3

2 4 6 8 10 9 7 5 3 1

Typeset in Haarlemmer MT by Deanta Global Publishing Services, Chennai, India
Printed and bound in USA by Berryville Graphics Inc., Berryville, Virginia

Bloomsbury Publishing Plc makes every effort to ensure that the papers used in the manufacture
of our books are natural, recyclable products made from wood grown in well-managed forests.
Our manufacturing processes conform to the environmental regulations of the country of origin.

To find out more about our authors and books visit www.bloomsbury.com and
sign up for our newsletters

For Pippin and Paul, to tell the story of a voyage they were too young to remember, and in memory of our dear friend and intrepid sailor, Peter Hancock.

CONTENTS

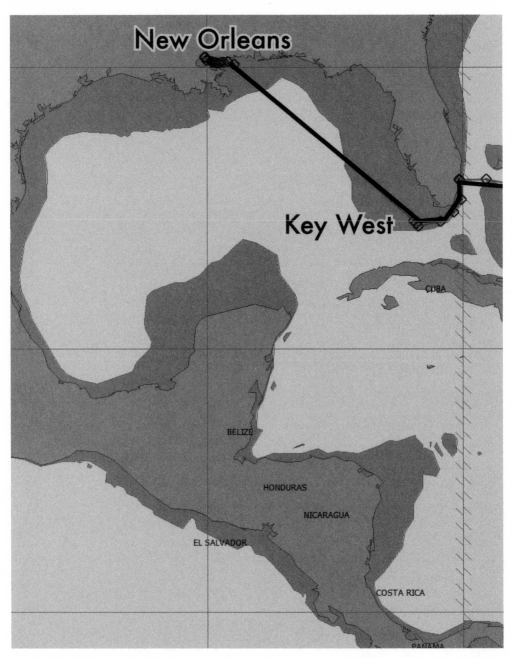

Track of *Nada* from Mandeville, Louisiana, to Cumana, Venezuela, January to June 1987.

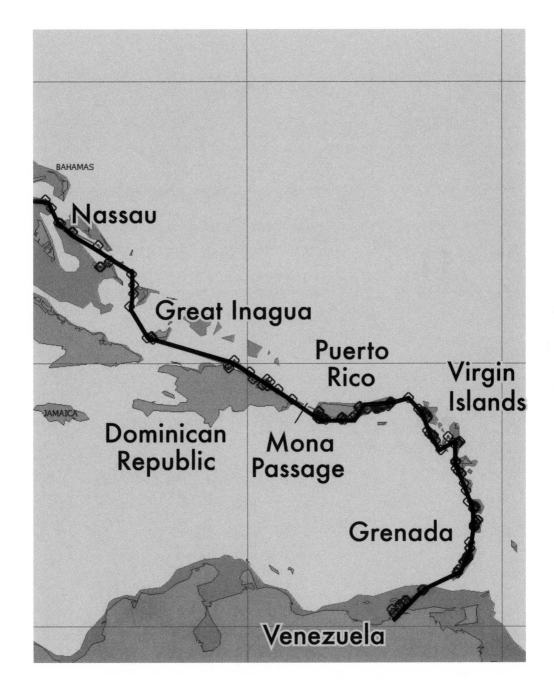

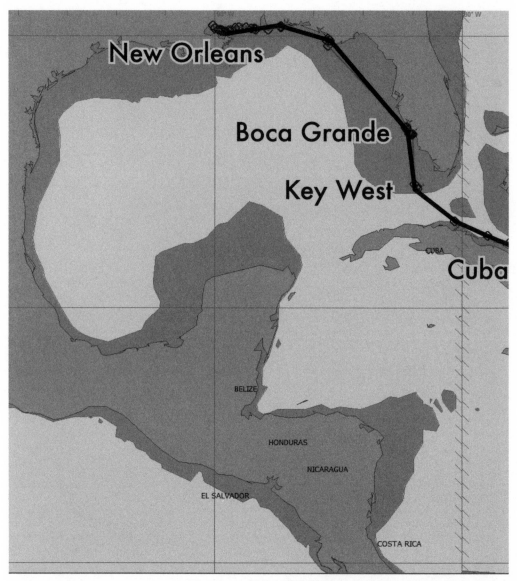

Nada's return track, from Cumana, Venezuela, to Mandeville, Louisiana, December 1987 to June 1988.

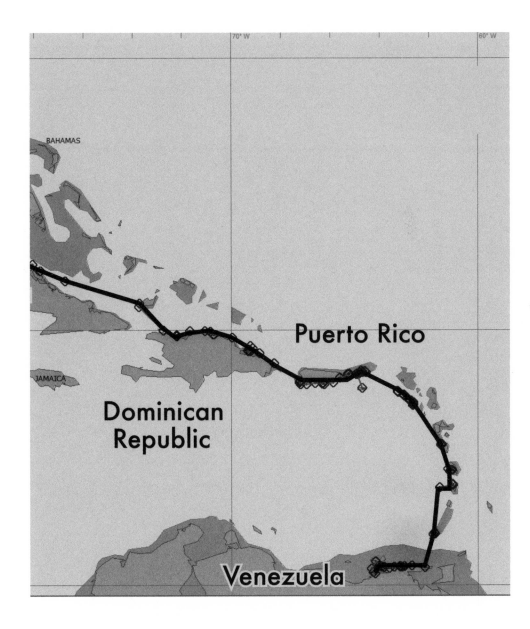

FOREWORD (2018)

I WROTE THIS BOOK, describing my family's first long cruise, in 1987–8, thirty years ago. It sat in a filing cabinet until I recently came across it and dusted it off. It catches us at a turning point in our lives when Terrie and I are starting a family and I am just beginning to make my mark as a marine technical writer. We have recently finished building our "dream" boat and are setting off as inexperienced, impecunious cruisers, driven by a love of adventure and a sense of optimism to explore the world. We have a lot to learn!

It is remarkable how much has changed in the succeeding three decades, but it is also remarkable how little has changed.

Perhaps nothing has changed more than navigational processes. In 1987 we were in the twilight of sextant-based navigation and at the dawn of recreational electronic positioning. We had a sextant and sight tables on board, and knew how to use them (I could not today), but also a first generation satellite navigation (satnav) system. It gave us intermittent fixes, often hours apart, that were generally accurate but sometimes wildly erroneous. There was no such thing as digital cartography—all plotting was done on paper charts, most of which were based on surveys from the 1800s and very few of which carried precise inshore detail. I still have those charts—looking at them today I am amazed that more cruising boats were not lost. Most coastal navigation was carried out with the help of a hand bearing compass (which I still use) and early cruising guides.

Shakedown Cruise is suffused with anxious nights sailing through rock- and reef-strewn waters, unsure of our precise position. On longer passages, such as across the Gulf of Mexico, we would sometimes deliberately aim a mile or two to one or other side of our intended landfall so that if we did not recognize where we were when we sighted land we would at least know which way to turn. This is a far cry from today, when we at all times know our position, often to within six feet, with it constantly plotted and updated in real time on digital charts. Between then and now we have lived through an astonishing technological shift that is not even remotely comparable to any previous advancements in the art of navigation.

In 1987 we were also at a point in time when lifestyles on board cruising boats were transitioning from camping out to an ever-closer approximation to living at home. We had a fridge and freezer (although I went through three systems before we achieved something reasonably efficient and effective), hot and cold running water (but only after running the engine to heat the water), and, in terms of those days, a moderately powerful electrical system built around a high-output alternator and a relatively large battery bank. We even had a microwave (although most of the time we did not have the energy to run it and instead used it as a bread storage bin!). This was luxurious cruising. Today these things are simply taken for granted.

In the pages of this book we frequently have trouble setting our anchor in the thin-sand-over-rock found in many Caribbean anchorages. The CQR was the default anchor within the cruising community. We also had a Danforth anchor as a "lunch" hook and a bronze fisherman anchor as a backup (we still have it). The modern generation of scoop anchors—the Spade, Rocna, Manson, Ultra, Mantus—are qualitatively better than anything available to us in 1987, removing one more anxiety from the cruising life. When the wind pipes up we sleep easy these nights in a way that we never could in the past.

Throughout *Shakedown Cruise* I am troubled by problems with my back (I did some damage working in the oilfields many years ago). Other technologies have now taken much of the hard work out of sailing, notably roller furling sails, electric winches, electric windlasses (ours was manual), and bow thrusters. We have them all on our current boat. *Nada*, the boat we sail in these pages, was ketch-rigged to break up the sail plan into smaller and more manageable areas. The genoa on our current boat has more sail area than all of *Nada*'s basic sails put together. We control the genoa at the push of a button. Whereas a 40-foot boat was considered a large cruising boat for two people to handle in 1987, today boats over 50 feet are commonplace.

Then there is the boat itself. We built *Nada* toward the end of the 1970s home-built era. There was already a vigorous debate concerning the relative merits for offshore cruising of traditional long-keeled, narrow beam, heavy displacement, double-ended boats versus lighter fin-keeled, wider beam, transom boats. I read every book available and came down on the traditional side. We then overbuilt *Nada*, especially the deck. The result was a relatively slow and tender boat with poor windward performance. This comes through in every chapter of *Shakedown Cruise*—we constantly struggle to make headway upwind and sometimes give up. On the other hand, *Nada* could take anything the weather gods could throw at us and never once—in all the tens of thousands of miles we put under her keel—pounded when coming off a wave. Although still conservative, our subsequent boats have looked less and less like *Nada*. Performance has improved considerably with no loss of safety or comfort. Unlike most modern boats, we still don't pound.

There is a substantial downside to the technological advances. Sailing has become expensive and prone to system failures. We are in danger of losing sight of why we go cruising. And in these pages there are some eternal themes that hold true as strongly today as they did for us in 1987. It is why Terrie and I are still cruising together.

There is the freedom that comes from casting off and heading out to sea. Once away from the dock you are in your own little universe, accountable to no one but yourself. In our increasingly regulated world there are not many mechanisms for achieving this, and none more effective than cruising. There is the sense of adventure and the desire to explore, traits deeply embedded in the DNA of all of us that have driven mankind to sail over the horizon since the dawn of history. There is the excitement of discovering new places, especially those inaccessible by any other means. There are the wonders of nature experienced, from sailing in company with humpback whales in the Dominican Republic, to enjoying a tropical sunset in a pristine Caribbean anchorage, to watching puffins hop in and out of their burrows on a Hebridean island.

From a cruising perspective, the world has become a much smaller and unsafe place since 1987. There are entire regions that were regularly cruised then to which we would not even consider sailing today. The western Caribbean itself is far more crowded, there are fewer places where anchoring is permitted, major resort developments have scarred many of the formerly pristine bays, and petty crime is up. But there are still vast regions of the world to be explored, full of natural wonders and welcoming people. These past several summers we have sailed the west coasts of Scotland and Ireland and as far north as the Faroes. In spite of the generally awful weather, we have enjoyed ourselves more than in any other region in which we have cruised. Old age and infirmity will put an end to our cruising before we run out of places to explore.

There are other timeless lessons here with respect to personal relationships, the tug of war between work and pleasure, and whether or not it is fair to uproot children and drag them along on a nomadic life.

In many ways it is remarkable that Terrie and I continue to cruise together, and in fact are even together at all, because she has never enjoyed sailing! It is partly her susceptibility to seasickness but mostly the fact that the act and challenge of sailing have simply not grabbed her interest. I had thought at the beginning of *Nada*'s cruise that over time she would come to love it, but this never happened. This is not uncommon among cruising couples where one partner is often the driving force and the other may well be there reluctantly at best. It frequently wrecks relationships. Even after all these years and miles under various keels, Terrie still does not like to sail.

What we learned during the course of this cruise was how to meld my love of sailing with Terrie's love of adventure, exploration, and the natural world. Over the course of 18 months we worked our way to an effective compromise: we keep the passages as short as is necessary to carry us to fabulous parts of the world. It's a formula that has worked for us ever since.

We were lucky in as much as neither of us had a career that we had to put on hold to go cruising. My back had put me out of the oilfield business and I was just beginning to get some traction with my writing. The cruising experience was a necessary and critical part of advancing this career, while Terrie, the artist, can find something she wants to paint pretty much any place we go. The pieces fit together in a way back then that they rarely did for other cruising sailors. Today, with modern communications, there are many careers that can be continued while cruising.

We took off with our one-year-old daughter, Pippin, and with Terrie three months pregnant. Our families thought we were crazy. *Shakedown Cruise* captures these months as Terrie became increasingly large, giving birth in late summer 1987; we then continued sailing several more months until summer 1988.

After Paul turned one—where *Shakedown Cruise* ends—we did get off the boat for 18 months until we had them both out of diapers and potty trained, but then we went back to sea, typically for 6 months or more a year, moving ashore and laying up *Nada* during hurricane season. Terrie home-schooled Pippin and Paul up to about age 12, at which point we did not feel competent to do this anymore and put them into regular school. When on the boat I tried to make Terrie and the children follow the Calvert home-school curriculum— at the time the predominant one used by cruising families. It was a mistake.

Children learn far more simply by being on boats and going to the places they go to, and by having the experiences they have, than they can ever learn through any curriculum. Anything they miss in terms of a formal education they will catch up in five minutes when the time comes. Both Pippin and Paul secured near full scholarships to high-end colleges. They have never had any problem making friends and socializing. Pippin is now 32 and Paul is 30. We all get along wonderfully; our family is closer than any other family we know. This too I put down to taking them to sea. Take those children and grandchildren sailing!

If you feel the salt water stirring in your veins, you should heed the call, sooner rather than later. Terrie and I have had a wonderful life; we wish the same for you.

Newcastle, Maine

FOREWORD (1988)

TERRIE AND I RECENTLY moved ashore into a cramped two-bedroom house in a working class neighborhood of similar small houses. We chose the house for its fenced-in backyard, which we naively thought would contain Pippin (two and a half) and Paul (one). It was even less successful than the netting around the lifelines on our 39-foot ketch *Nada*. Before we had the first truckload of gear from the boat unpacked, Pippin and Paul were out front surrounded by curious children. Pippin, unaccustomed to clothes after two years in the tropics, stripped naked and paraded up and down the street. Next she invited everyone to come in the house and jump on her bed—never having had one before, the old double box spring we had borrowed was a great novelty to her. Soon there was a riot going on in her room: these children never got this kind of license at home! Shortly thereafter various elder brothers and sisters arrived to collect their younger siblings. It was to be weeks before any of them were allowed near us again.

Meantime we continued unpacking. It's hard to believe, but as we stripped the boat we ran out of space in the house to store all our accumulated junk. Sails, a sewing machine and bedding; tools, oxyacetylene cylinders, and rolls of copper tubing; life vests, life rings, and strobe lights; hundreds, no thousands, of feet of assorted rope; a pile of charts 15 inches deep; a dozen of Terrie's framed watercolors, plus masses of art supplies; my typewriter and two large boxes of boat equipment manuals (the raw material for a couple of books); snorkels, fins, buckets and spades; masks and statues from the Dominican Republic; bottles of rum from the Virgin Islands and Antigua; termite-eaten baskets from Haiti; spices from Grenada; Christmas ornaments from Venezuela; and endless odds and ends. Our boat, *Nada*, rose four inches to reveal her waterline for the first time in a couple of years. How on earth had we stowed all this? No wonder we could never keep *Nada* tidy.

We've been sifting through our oddments and reliving old memories ever since.

Hammond, Louisiana

IT IS JANUARY 1987. After years of dreaming and hard work, we are setting sail on our home-built boat, *Nada*, from Mandeville, Louisiana, for the South Pacific. The first leg of our journey will take us some 600 miles across the Gulf of Mexico to Key West.

It is just past midnight on a crisp, clear, moonlit night when we cast off our mooring lines and maneuver out of our slip. In the dark we forget to unplug the shorepower cable: we rip it in half and find the torn end trailing overboard in the morning, an apt symbol of the rough cutting of our umbilical cord since we are leaving much unfinished business behind.

In these pre-Katrina days, before the storm surge wreaked its havoc, Mandeville's waterfront is dominated by stately nineteenth century vacation homes lining the north shore of Lake Ponchartrain. The town's raison d'être is a small harbor on Bayou Castine. In bygone days steamboats with bands playing and flags flying brought the rich and famous across from New Orleans on summer weekends to escape the city. Bayou Castine now divides Mandeville from the surrounding cypress swamp with its egrets, nutrias, and snakes, all of which have been frequent visitors to our slip.

We are barely underway when the engine splutters and dies. We drift slowly down the bayou in the dark with the crew—Terrie, who is three months pregnant, and two friends, Ray and Lyle, whom we have recruited for the passage to Key West—standing by, ready to fend off the banks and other boats. Our one-year old daughter, Pippin, is asleep, tucked in behind a leecloth on a berth in the saloon.

I scramble below to diagnose the problem—air in the fuel supply—and then bleed the fuel system to get us going again. We motor through sleepy Mandeville harbor and into Lake Ponchartrain where we find no wind and hardly a ripple on the water. The engine-driven refrigeration system chooses this time to pack up. Terrie takes the helm while I find and fix a jammed impeller on the condenser cooling pump.

We chug steadily eastward toward the Gulf of Mexico with Lake Ponchartrain shimmering in the moonlight. The mast-mounted steaming light quits, and then the stern light. I decide we can make do with the masthead tri-color light until we arrive in Key West. Shortly thereafter a seal on the toilet springs a leak, dribbling raw sewage into the boat. Yuck!

Someone suggests it is time to read the omens and turn back. Ever since I first sailed a dinghy at a Church of England summer camp—at age twelve—I have wanted to go sailing. A friend and I persuaded our school to let us opt out of regular sports on Wednesday afternoons to sail his father's dinghy on a local flooded gravel pit. During my teen years the first singlehanded round-the-world race made headline news and fueled a generation of wannabe cruisers. I am one of these. I have read every book written by seminal cruising sailors such as the Hiscocks and Roths. I am not turning back.

We have been making final preparations and accumulating supplies for months. Every locker on *Nada* is packed to bursting with stores and spare parts. These include a sewing machine, a complete spare variable pitch propeller unit, an oxyacetylene kit, and a refrigeration vacuum pump. There is nothing that has failed so far that I cannot fix along the way.

Terrie is a far less enthusiastic sailor; her passion has always been making art. We met in Oxford, England, where her father, a Pentagon-based colonel in the U.S. Air Force was attending—with his family in tow—a NATO conference on counterinsurgency warfare. I was heavily involved in the local anti-Vietnam war movement. I happened to know (from my university days— I had the previous year been studying for an MSc in Strategic Studies) one of the presenters at the conference who thought it would be funny to set me up. He called me: "Nigel, you want to come get pissed for free?" "Of course!"

I show up at a NATO reception in a pair of bright red velvet bell-bottom trousers with hair well below my shoulders. Terrie is nineteen, a wild American teenager beyond any form of parental control and by now thoroughly bored with her stay in England. As soon as she sees me she comes over, tells me to hang on for a couple of minutes, disappears and returns in a scruffy pair of jeans. We take off for the pub. It is to be many years before her family accepts me while my mother tells me I "got what I deserved"!

Terrie is way more exciting than any English girlfriend I have known. I am keen to impress her. I suggest we "borrow" *Wallop*, my elder brother's 28-foot wooden sailboat (he is conveniently in Canada and so well out of the way) based on the east coast of England, and go sailing for the weekend. We round up a crew and fill the bilges with bottles of home-made beer. Then Terrie says: "Why don't we go to Amsterdam?" I have no more than the most basic knowledge of how to navigate, and the only chart we have of the other side of the North Sea is a small-scale one pre-dating the Second World War, but I am not going to admit I don't know how to get us there. We make it to Amsterdam, with Terrie seasick much of the way. On the return voyage we are run down by a ship while becalmed—no wind whatsoever and hardly a ripple on the water—with not enough time to start our temperamental hand-cranked engine to get out of the way.

We can see the ship is going to plow into us but there is nothing we can do; it hits us close to the stern, spinning *Wallop* around and throwing the crew across the boat. Our wooden transom is driven sideways, carrying the planking on both sides with it, just above the waterline. We crash and bang along the length of the ship—remarkably, the mast does not come down— and bounce through its stern wave, coming to rest in calm waters with the last of the ship's wake gurgling through the open holes on both sides of *Wallop*. There are five of us on board; we are lucky to be alive and to not lose *Wallop*.

I cannot get Terrie near sailboats for years, so we build a couple of canal boats (narrowboats) in England and live on them through most of the 1970s.

I find work on the assembly line in a car factory to pay for the repairs to *Wallop*, and for the first of the narrowboats. At one point I am elected as the shop steward (union organizer) for my section of the factory. It is a turbulent time in the British car industry, which is essentially bankrupt in the face of foreign competition, with management attempting to rectify the situation on the backs of the workforce. We are frequently on strike. The company eventually breaks the union.

We cannot afford an engine for the first of the canal boats so I buy a junked Perkins 4-107 diesel from the local scrap yard, sign up for a British government course that trains farmers in how to maintain their tractor engines, and donate the Perkins as a class project. The class completely disassembles and rebuilds the engine—pistons, rings, bearings, valves, the whole nine yards—and we end up with, for all intents and purposes, a new engine for free! It is my introduction to diesel engines.

While building the narrowboats Terrie and I find we work well together and neither of us minds living in the middle of a construction site. In fact, in one way or another pretty much since we met (it is now 47 years) we have always lived in a construction site, whether it is the next boat or house. I do the basic structural work, with help from Terrie when necessary; Terrie comes behind me, hides my mistakes, and makes what we do look beautiful. It is the artist in her.

While still living in England, I eventually persuade Terrie to reconsider an ocean-going sailboat. I am looking at a 38-foot Bruce Roberts design for home-built steel boats. We have a friend who is an excellent welder. However, Terrie is homesick, so before we order the plans we visit Louisiana, the home of her grandparents. It is 1978 and the oil industry is booming; I discover I can earn three times as much as I am in England, working on offshore oil production platforms in the Gulf of Mexico.

I bribe my way into a job as an oilfield mechanic and electrician. Although I have fooled around with motorcycles and cars since my early teens, and have had some limited work experience with industrial scale engines, I have no electrical background and no familiarity with most of the equipment in the oilfields. Because of the expense of sending labor and parts out to the rigs and production platforms, when things go wrong we are expected to have a go at fixing them regardless of whether or not we understand the equipment or problem; if we break whatever it is, the company sends a new one. Over the next six years I break a lot of expensive equipment and in the process learn a great deal.

We move into an 11-foot by 11-foot cabin on Terrie's grandfather's property, with a toilet and sink in one corner and a foldout couch as a bed that occupies half the cabin when deployed. We eat with Terrie's parents who have built their retirement house on another part of the property. We do not discuss the Vietnam War.

This is the era of home-built cruising boats. Ferenc Maté's book, *From a Bare Hull*, has sold 250,000 copies. In that book he describes the 39-foot William-Atkin-designed *Ingrid* as the ultimate cruising boat. I have a check in an envelope ready to mail to Bruce Roberts when I come across this passage. I tear up the check and order a bare Ingrid hull—a big plastic bathtub with one bulkhead bonded in place to keep the sides from splaying out—from Jerry Husted at Bluewater Boats in Washington state; there is no deck, no ballast, no interior—nothing but the bare hull.

We knock the end out of a barn owned by Terrie's grandfather and extend the barn with a plastic-covered frame. The hull arrives and is maneuvered into place with a come-along, using lengths of metal pipe as rollers. Terrie and I cannot agree on a name for the boat, so call her *Nada*, which is Spanish for "nothing"; all our subsequent boats have been *Nadas* (we are currently on *Nada IV*—see sidebar later in this chapter). We work on *Nada* under that plastic awning in the heat and humidity of Louisiana summers; when I am laying up fiberglass there is a trail of white spots where the sweat has dripped off the hem of my T-shirt. It takes a six-pack to rehydrate each evening.

My offshore job is a week on and a week off, giving me 26 weeks a year to work on the boat. While I am offshore, Terrie concentrates on her artwork, which has been the one constant in her life, including through her wild teen years. She can capture a likeness in a few strokes. She becomes passionate about creating complex woodblock prints, which require incredible focus and attention to detail in the carving process. She is creating large multi-block prints that take hundreds of hours to carve; at times I find her hunched over her carving table asleep. The first attempts to pull a print are always stressful with the various blocks not registering properly and a worn-out Terrie becoming emotional. She is creating some amazing work and building up a small but devoted local following.

Over the course of the next six years we do everything from casting the lead for *Nada*'s keel to building the deck and interior and installing the systems, including building the fridge and freezer system through a process of trial and error (there is almost no technical information available to boatowners and

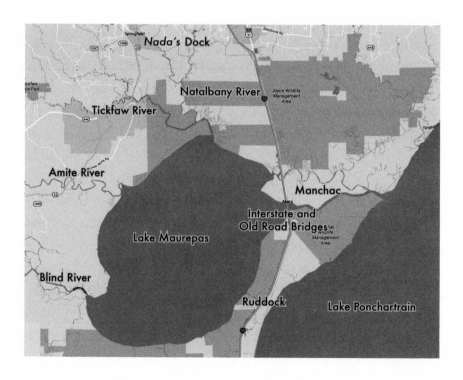

boatbuilders such as ourselves). I spend a fair bit of time in the local university library reading every refrigeration book available.

Once we have evolved a working refrigerator and freezer, and I understand what is making it work as opposed to our previous efforts, I decide this information would be useful to other boaters. I write and self-publish a book on marine refrigeration systems. It is a financial failure and the last time I try self-publishing! It does, however, open the door for me to International Marine; I am asked to write *Marine Diesel Engines*. Meantime, we are able to fund the build process for *Nada* from my wages as we go along.

We launch *Nada* in 1982 and continue working on her, and fitting her out, alongside a dock in the midst of a small cypress swamp on the Natalbany River, in Louisiana, close to where we are living. Our initial sailing trials are in shallow Lake Maurepas, which empties into the western end of Lake Ponchartrain. On our very first sail my log notes: "Caught in squall gusting to 40 knots with main, jib, staysail, and mizzen up. No one on board with any sailing experience except Nigel. Mainsail slides jam. Boat knocked down. Breidart head (the chimney for our wood/coal stove) and two (separate!) shoes lost overboard. Return to dock and grease all sail slides."

Our trials and tribulations continue. The next few log entries read:

> "Charlie pulls main halyard cleat off main mast. Return to dock and remake all cleats and winch bases with epoxy and machine screws."

> "Fine run to Blind River but run aground in mouth of river. Greg swims out an anchor and we winch off."

> "Strong winds. Spend night anchored near Manchac. Next day winds 32-40 knots. Lose dinghy and have some trouble recovering it (seat torn out). Doing over 6 knots under mizzen and staysail. Cabin side goes under water—portholes open!"

We decide it is time to explore farther afield. At Pass Manchac between lakes Maurepas and Ponchartrain there is a two-span interstate bridge and the old highway bridge. I had assumed they would be high enough for us to motor under but when we arrive there we discover they are not. Unless we take the mast down, it looks as if our round-the-world cruising boat is trapped in twelve-mile-diameter Lake Maurepas! We lay *Nada* up against the pilings that define the channel under the bridges and I go to the masthead to see if I can use the leverage of the mast to drag *Nada* over sideways sufficiently to fit under the bridges. "Try to get under Manchac Bridge—Nigel at masthead with navigation light removed. Make it under interstate bridges with 8 inches to clear, but need another 12 inches on old road bridge (water level at 50 feet mark)." We return to Lake Maurepas.

"Feb. 6 1983: Good day's sailing (20-knot winds). Problem mooring up due to wind and current: get stuck on Colonel Mathew's cypress tree."

"Feb. 20: 25–30 knot winds. Close-hauled (tacking) to Tickfaw. Tack too late and run aground on lee shore after mistaking Amite beacon for Tickfaw beacon. Have to strip off and swim out an anchor to winch off."

"March 4: 20–30 knot winds. Close-hauled (tacking) to Blind River. Jib sets very badly—overpowers boat. Run back to Tickfaw under down wind poles at steady 6–7 knots. Find knotmeter under reads by almost 20%."

"April 1: Left at 5.00 pm. Winds gusting to 30 knots even in river. Blowing from south at sustained Force 8 in lake with 3 foot chop—just about stops *Nada* dead. Power out with mizzen only and make anchorage somewhere around Ruddock around 11 pm. Winds increase to over 40 knots and seas pick up to 4–5 feet with many breaking. Boat riding hard on 100 feet of chain— breaks anchor windlass main shaft. All the chain runs out and is only stopped by bitter end shackled to bulkhead (midnight). Anchor dragging previous to this but holds on bitter end shackle now. Fairly close to shore and then wind swings around to west making it a lee shore. Bowsprit alternately completely buried in the water and 10 feet in air. Greg and Nigel both seasick. Unable to repair winch. Ride out a sleepless night. Lull around 4.00 am to 15–20 knots and seas calm to 3 feet but begin to pick up again around 5.30 am and veering to southwest. Manage to get anchor and chain back on board by hand and sail under mizzen and staysail at speeds up to 7.5 knots back to Tickfaw (winds 25–30 knots again). At some point staysail outhaul tears off boom at back and breaks in half. Back at landing at 9.30 am!"

"April 16/17: Go out overnight. Broad reach to Blind River and stay the night. Explore mile or two up the river next day and downwind sail back to Tickfaw—6 knots in 10–12 knot winds. Very pleasant!"

By 1984 we are finally ready to test all systems in the open ocean. We pick a day when the water level in Lake Maurepas is unusually low, lay *Nada* up against the bridge pilings once again, and work our way under the two spans of the interstate bridge and the single span of the old highway bridge into Lake Ponchartrain. We have a pleasant sail to a new berth up Bayou Castine in Mandeville. Over the course of the next two years we test *Nada* and her systems in two extended open-water passages—during my annual three-week vacation break—across the 500-mile-wide Gulf of Mexico to the Yucatan Peninsula in Mexico and back.

In the meantime, the oilfield job almost kills me on several occasions (I still bear the scars from one of the fires). The first two mechanics I work with are both injured so badly that neither ever returns to work. Just before I sign on, three women walk into the company offices in New Orleans and threaten to file a discrimination suit because there are no female employees offshore. The company promptly hires all three and throws them into the bunkhouses with the rest of us with no separate bedrooms or bathrooms. They stick it out but eventually all three are seriously hurt. After six years, my offshore career is ended by two ruptured discs in my back which have given me problems ever since, but by then *Nada* is paid for…

As we are readying *Nada*, some of Terrie's relatives would like to complete the damage the oilfield has done! They attempt to seize her grandfather's assets and hide him in a nasty nursing home under a false name. When we find him and file to recover his assets so we can put him in a decent home our little house is shot up (Terrie has a number of prints hanging up to dry which have bullet holes through them), I am threatened at gunpoint and assaulted, Terrie is subjected to obscene phone calls and death threats while I am offshore, threats are made to poison our well, and friends visiting us have guns trained on them as they come in and out of our driveway. *Nada* is vandalized. We get to know way more about the Louisiana legal system and the mechanisms of local law (un)enforcement than we ever want to. Before it is all over Terrie's grandfather dies, the lawyers carve up most of his estate between them, and Terrie's father's house burns to the ground in suspicious circumstances. It is one reason we now live in Maine.

On both our earlier trips to the Yucatan Terrie struggles with seasickness and I also succumb from time to time. She shows little interest in the mechanics of sailing and navigation, but thoroughly enjoys the destinations, in particular exploring Mayan ruins in the Yucatan; travel and a love of adventure are part of her DNA.

Now, in 1987, as we motor eastward through Lake Ponchartrain at the start of our liveaboard cruising life I feel sure we can conquer the seasickness and am convinced that once we settle into exploration mode she will grow to enjoy the sailing as well as the lifestyle (I am wrong about this). We will, in any case, have to make extended layovers in various cruising destinations as we are short on funds and I will have to supplement these through my writings, which are just now beginning to produce income with the publication of *Marine Diesel Engines*. These layovers will provide the opportunity for Terrie to explore ashore and paint.

We plan to cruise in a broad arc through the Caribbean, taking in most of the West Indies and the northern coast of South America before transiting the Panama Canal and following the "milk run" to the South Pacific: the Galapagos, the Marquesas, the Society Islands, including the fabled Tahiti, and on to New Zealand. We had reckoned on leaving in November and are already months behind our planned departure date. Our baby is due in July. We need to have *Nada* safely below latitude 11 degrees north, south of the Caribbean hurricane belt, before the onset of hurricane season at the end of June; if there are any complications with the birth, this will enable us to leave *Nada* without worry.

We press on toward the eastern end of Lake Ponchartain, with its lift and swing bridges. On two previous night exits we were forced to climb the girders of the massive bridge structures to wake the bridge operators in order to get the bridges opened, but this time we pass through without a hitch.

The wintertime night air cools and a patchy fog settles on the surface of the water, obscuring the range lights for the narrow channel beyond the bridges, a passage we have successfully made in the dark on a number of previous occasions. But this time the tide pushes us out of the channel and at 0500 we run aground on a falling tide.

We hurriedly launch our home-built cold-molded wooden dinghy. I row out an anchor and drop it in the channel, a mere boat length away. Ray and Lyle set to work cranking on the manual anchor windlass. With considerable enthusiasm they drag us onto a narrow spoil bank between *Nada* and the channel. Daybreak finds our 6-foot draft boat in 4½ feet of water and stuck fast in the mud: some start to a dream cruise!

I do what I should have done in the first place—take the dinghy and pole around to check depths. It does not take long to realize that we will have to go out the way we came in. We set a stern anchor and another off to the side. Ray dons scuba gear and tries to recover the main anchor, but we have pulled it in so deep it is immovable. We buoy it, cast it loose, and push it to the back of our minds to concentrate on the main problem: getting off. To lessen our draft we take the mainsail halyard to the side anchor and haul the boat down by the masthead until the deck is underwater, a tactic I had read about but not yet tried. We crank and crank at the stern anchor until the line is bar taut and the crew running out of steam. In spite of rolling the side decks under, we haven't moved an inch: muddy Ponchartrain has us firmly in her grasp.

A young man motors by in a shrimp boat. We persuade him to tie onto the mainsail halyard and pull us from the side. I jump aboard his boat and he throttles up. *Nada* rolls over and once again the side deck goes under. The crew is standing on the inside of the cockpit coamings and hanging onto the rigging and mast to keep from falling out of the cockpit; Terrie is hanging onto Pippin. The shrimper jerks back his throttles. "Give it more gas!" I yell. "It'll roll over," he shouts back. We take a short break while I give him a brief explanation of the nature of ballast keels and stability on sailboats.

The shrimper maneuvers back into position, takes up the slack, and guns his engines. The rail rolls under; the side deck goes under; the portholes in the

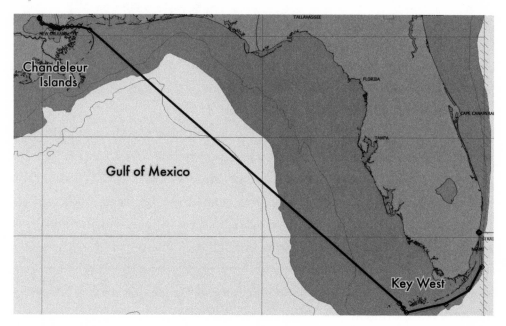

cabin side begin to go under. He pulls back his throttles. "More gas; more gas," I cry. "My knees are turning to jelly!" "It's my boat; you let me worry about it." And so finally he gives it the gas, the portholes go halfway under, the crew hangs on tightly, and *Nada* slowly comes free. We use his power winches to recover all three anchors and are ready to move on again; dragging off by the masthead clearly works! It's a lesson we remember—years later, on several occasions we beg a tow from passing fishing boats when we ground hard during the process of researching cruising guides to the northwest Caribbean and Cuba. Although as we grow older we have become more cautious in our explorations and run aground less often, nevertheless as late as 2016 we end up high and dry when hiding from a gale up a tidal river on the wild Atlantic coast of Ireland!

We foul the bottom once more in Lake Ponchartrain, having to kedge off, before regaining the channel. This escapade costs us seven hours.

There is still no wind. We motor through the Rigolets, the channel that links Lake Ponchartrain with the Gulf of Mexico. We pick up a little breeze from the northeast in the Mississippi Sound beyond the Rigolets, motorsailing through the twisting channels between the numerous sandbanks. Dusk finds us approaching Cat Island, in the low-lying chain of sandy barrier islands protecting the Mississippi coastline. We clear the Chandeleur Islands, the last of the islands, during the night, entering the open waters of the Gulf of Mexico at last. We have a light breeze from the south. In the early hours of the morning the wind veers to the northwest and then north, and we are finally able to shut down the engine and reach eastward. We are on our way.

RUNNING AGROUND AND KEDGING OFF

Some people seem to think running aground is a tremendous indignity. Over the years we have come to think that if we don't run aground at least periodically, we are likely missing some excellent gunkholing possibilities! However, we only adopt this somewhat cavalier attitude in non-threatening situations (primarily, no wind and waves, and preferably minimal tide).

When you run aground on a hard bottom it is immediately apparent— there will be a series of hard knocks. On a soft bottom, the boat may just loose speed—it may take a moment to realize what is happening.

If you are close hauled or close reaching under sail, tacking immediately, leaving the headsail sheeted on the old tack, will back the headsail, driving the head around and causing the boat to heel, which will lessen its draft. With any luck, you will sail straight off. On any other point of sail (a reach or a run) it is almost always best to let go the sheets and get the sails down as quickly as possible. Make a quick check for any trailing lines, shorten the dinghy painter if the dinghy is being towed astern, and then crank the engine and give it full reverse. With any luck, the boat will back off.

If you are still stuck, keep the engine in reverse while the crew rushes rhythmically from one side of the boat to the other, setting it rolling from side to side. Sometimes the combined effect of this together with the reverse prop wash being driven under the keel is enough to break the grip of soft bottoms and get the boat moving. If the boat has a regular keel (not a wing keel, or twin bilge keels) you can swing the boom out until it comes up against the shrouds, tie it off in this position, and then have the crew work their way as far outboard as possible. This will heel most boats quite considerably, hopefully lessening the draft enough to power off. Note that heeling a boat to reduce its draft will not work with wing keels and twin bilge keels; the draft actually increases with heeling.

Another method we have used, on occasion, to induce heeling: we have set our boom over the side, lashed it in place, set up the topping lift, and hung all kinds of heavy objects from its end (including the dinghy suspended with a cat's cradle of rigging, and pumped partially full of water). Using an anchor to pull the boat down by the masthead is also extremely effective. The farther off the anchor can be set, and the lower the masthead can be pulled, the more the horizontal force that will be exerted, which will also help to drag the boat off sideways. If the boat's head can be pulled around until the wind is at least abeam, and preferably forward of the beam, the sails can be set and oversheeted to impart both heeling and drive in the desired direction.

If these measures fail you had better throttle back the engine before you suck a load of sand and/or silt into the cooling system and cause it to overheat. It is time to try something else.

If you have run aground in tidal waters, first determine if the tide is coming in or going out. If it is coming in, it is just a matter of waiting for it to lift you off. However, if the wind and waves are driving you further aground, it is imperative to launch the dinghy and row out a kedge anchor as soon as possible. Row this out to a point well beyond where you want it to set, pitch the anchor and rode overboard, and then return to the boat to crank in the rode until it is taut. A kedge anchor should always be set on a *very long rode*. This is to give it some dragging room in which to set, and to ensure that as the boat comes off and the rode shortens there is still adequate scope to maintain the set and keep the anchor from breaking out.

When considering your options, don't forget that the most powerful winch on a boat is often the cockpit genoa sheet winch and not the windlass. The best course of action may well be to lay out a stern anchor, bringing the rode on board through a stern fairlead to a cockpit winch. Alternatively, once the windlass is loaded up, use a running hitch to attach a line to the rode somewhere forward of the windlass, and then take this line to a winch and crank in on it to assist the windlass. Remember that a well-tensioned rode is a potentially dangerous beast. The most likely point at which it will break is where it comes aboard, so figure its maximum snapback range if it breaks at this point, and keep everyone out of range.

If you run aground on a falling tide, you may have just a few minutes to get off, using any of the methods already suggested. If these fail, you are going to have to wait for the next rising tide. If the tide range is more than a few feet, and you run aground at much above low tide, you will probably dry out. There is much that needs attention:

- The first thing is to make sure that the boat leans toward the side on which the bottom slopes upward. If the boat goes down the other way, it will lie at an extreme angle of heel and may well flood when the tide comes back in.
- If necessary, to make sure that the boat goes down the right way, set the boom over this side of the boat and have the crew hang from it to provide the necessary heeling.
- If this fails, set an anchor off to the side on which you want the boat to go down, bring its rode up to the end of the main halyard, and tie the halyard to it. Now tighten the halyard. This will pull the boat down by the masthead, exerting tremendous leverage. Note that if a boat has a fractional rig, there may be no shrouds providing lateral support to the head of the mast. In this case, it may be advisable to use the genoa halyard for pulling down by the masthead.
- Pump the bilge before the boat heels significantly so that the bilge water won't flood lockers.

- Cook a meal and then close the propane cylinder valves. The reason for this is that at an extreme angle of heel it is possible to get liquid propane entering the propane lines, which is potentially quite dangerous.

- Check to see that the batteries are properly secured. If you have wet cells, you may need to remove them and keep them more-or-less upright to prevent the acid leaking out.

- If the boat goes way over, the engine may start leaking oil out the dipstick tube or some other orifice—keep an eye on it and plug leaks as necessary. Fuel and water tank vents may also leak—pay especial attention to the fuel tank vents.

- As the boat approaches the point at which it will come to rest on the turn of the bilge, check for sharp rocks or an uneven bottom that may result in point loading. If necessary, use locker lids and even bagged sails to cushion the load.

- Wing keels can be a bit of a problem. The boat may try to stay upright, which is potentially very dangerous—it may subsequently crash over on its side when the tide is out. It should be pulled over, even at the risk of damaging the keel. If it is left upright, be sure to find a way to lash sturdy legs (such as a spinnaker pole) to it on both sides. Do everything you can to keep the boat as vertical as possible—this will minimize the load on the supports. For example, set out a couple of anchors (one on each side) connected to halyards so that you can use the leverage of the mast to keep the boat in position.

- Finally, either row out a kedge anchor as far off into deep water as your rode length will allow before the tide goes out, or walk an anchor out when the tide is down (if the bottom is soft, you will want to row it out before the tide goes out). Check its set by winching the rode taut.

If nothing you do gets you off, it is time to think about a tow.

The Gulf of Mexico can be a frustrating body of water in which to sail. The prevailing winds are from the southeast, the direction to Key West, our destination. *Nada* does not sail well to windward, partly because of the hull design, and partly because while building her we read various accounts of encountering the ultimate storm—such as that described by Miles and Beryl Smeeton in their book *Once is Enough*—and grossly overbuilt the deck to make it unnecessarily strong. *Nada* is top heavy: any time we are close-hauled in even a moderate breeze, the caprails and side decks are awash. We try hard to avoid upwind passages (on the plus side, without this tenderness we most likely would not have got *Nada* under the Manchac bridges)!

In the winter months cold fronts periodically force their way down from the Arctic and stall over the warm waters of the Gulf, generating northerly gales and nasty seas. My strategy is to exploit the favorable wind direction of a cold front and put up with the resulting rough conditions. *Nada* has been built to handle pretty much anything the weather gods can throw at her; the crew is the weak link.

We have set sail in January 1987 following the passage of an unusually strong cold front that has lashed Florida and the Keys with their worst storms in years, causing considerable flooding and damage. I am expecting large, disturbed seas, but hoping to catch a day or two of northerly and northeasterly winds that will drive us toward Key West. Instead, we find the seas have already more or less subsided and the winds are light and variable, leaving us motorsailing for hours at a time. We are forced to change our hanked-on headsails, and trim the sails and adjust our heading at frequent intervals. It is aggravating sailing.

GULF OF MEXICO COLD FRONTS

The prevailing winds in the Gulf of Mexico are from the southeast except during the winter months on those occasions when the jet stream dips southward from Canada. The jet stream spawns cold fronts that work their way from Texas across the entire Gulf of Mexico down to the north coast of Cuba, through Florida and the Keys, and across the Bahamas. Depending on how far south the jet stream dips, and how strong the cold front, the effects may be felt along the north coasts of Hispaniola and Puerto Rico all the way eastward to the Virgin Islands, temporarily stalling out the trade winds.

Cold fronts in these waters follow a predictable pattern. The front is preceded by a gradual change in wind direction from the southeast to the southwest, with the wind building typically to at least 25 knots and often to gale force and stronger. The front brings an advancing line of cumulonimbus clouds with sometimes violent squalls; there is a sudden wind shift into the northwest. The temperature drops dramatically, in extreme cases by as much as 50°F in less than an hour. The colder air behind the front generally brings clearing skies, although the front may trail further showers. Following the passage of the front the wind gradually eases and slowly veers through the north, northeast, and east back to the southeast.

These cold fronts begin to assert themselves in late November and December. By January and February there is often one a week and sometimes more. They continue to sweep across the Gulf of Mexico throughout the early months of the year, gradually declining in strength and numbers until the beginning of hurricane season in June. The more powerful the cold front and the slower it travels the harder the wind blows and the longer the wind remains in the northwest and north.

Given the poor windward performance of *Nada*, for our first Gulf of Mexico crossing in 1984 from Lake Ponchartrain to Isla Mujeres at the tip of the Yucatan Peninsula I settled on a strategy of leaving as a cold front came through. In a worst case—a weak, fast-moving cold front—this would give us two to three days of following winds in which to jump-start the 600-mile passage. In a best case we would get five days of powerful northerlies that would hold for the entire passage, and would reach as far south as the Yucatan.

For that first crossing I picked an extremely powerful cold front; the wind was blowing at and above gale force from start to finish. By the time we reached the shoaling waters off the Yucatan coastline, we had twenty foot and larger waves with substantial breaking crests. With a reefed mainsail and the jib held out with the downwind pole, *Nada* was surfing down the wave faces out of control. Even with our 7-foot tiller, and hauling on it with all my strength, I could not keep *Nada* from rounding up in the troughs. Knowing what I know today, I realize we were lucky not to have capsized. The final night of the passage the pole ripped off the mast and disappeared into the blackness, after which I took in some sail. We made it to Isla Mujeres in a little over four days, something we never again achieved in multiple crossings!

One day an Englishman, Peter Hancock, who became our dear friend but is now sadly deceased, pulled into the slip next to us in Mandeville after singlehanding his 26-foot Contessa across the Atlantic in order to attend his daughter's wedding in Baton Rouge. Peter, too, decided to explore the northwest Caribbean. I explained the cold front strategy to him. Peter recruited a crew, Daniel, the photographer from the wedding, for the trip. Daniel had never sailed before and naively thought it would be exciting to have an offshore experience.

Peter set sail just before Christmas in a record-breaking cold front that brought snow to New Orleans and put ice on the Mississippi River. We followed a week or so later and caught up with them in Isla Mujeres. There a distraught Daniel described the terrifying experience of being days out from land, seasick, in a howling gale with freezing rain, running under bare poles and dragging warps to slow down while Peter hung off the back of the boat repairing damaged steering gear. Periodically, waves broke over the stern, filling the cockpit and making their way below. At one point the floorboards in the cabin were awash. With the steering repaired, a drunk Peter was singing Christmas carols at the top of his voice while swigging gin from the bottle. (Peter was very fond of his gin.) Daniel flew home; I have a feeling Peter put him off sailing for life!

In these circumstances our just installed tiller-mounted autopilot is of limited, though much appreciated, use. But on day two a larger-than-usual wave drives the rudder over, breaking the autopilot mount on the tiller. After temporary repairs another wave breaks the mount in the cockpit. Following two more breakages and repairs water penetrates the actuator seals and locks up the mechanism. Penetrating fluid and Vise grips free things up, but later the main bearing disintegrates. This is not repairable: we are forced to steer by hand and reluctantly conclude that the unit does not have the power to handle the steering loads of our heavy ketch.

The wind works around to the southeast, putting us on a beat in short seas. Loaded down as *Nada* is she heels way over, taking on a most uncomfortable motion. Clothes and bedding—for which there is no room in overstuffed lockers—begin to fall about the cabin. Books fly out of the bookcase. A couple of portholes that have never leaked drip on the port and starboard berths. Terrie and Pippin are both seasick, with Terrie unwilling to take any medication because of her pregnancy. We knew about Terrie's susceptibility to seasickness but Pippin is a shock; we had read somewhere that babies are immune to *mal de mer*—we weren't expecting this.

Even without the seasickness Terrie is having a rough time. Pippin demands constant attention. She has not taken kindly to being on board and frequently lets us know with the most penetrating scream of any child we have known. In harbor or at anchor she can roam around the boat but at sea this is unsafe except in the calmest conditions. We end up holding her much of the time with the load falling mainly on Terrie since I am tied up with boat work. We learn to sail mostly at night so that Pippin sleeps through a good bit of it, but we never really come to terms with having a baby on board while sailing, probably because most of our trips are too short to establish a satisfactory routine.

Somewhere in the middle of the Gulf of Mexico we meet up with a lone trawler with onboard *radio fax*, a system for transmitting weather charts; we secure an updated weather forecast. A cold front from Texas is on its way across the Gulf. Our flagging spirits revive: the strong northwest winds associated with the front will put us on a downwind run to Key West.

When the front comes through we are once again motorsailing in light air with Terrie and Pippin recovered. The temperature drops sharply as the wind veers first to the west and then northwest, building rapidly to 25 knots. Within a few hours we are rolling and yawing downwind under a double-reefed main and poled-out jib in confused 6- to 8-foot seas, the occasional wave considerably larger, tearing along at hull speed, mother and baby seasick once again; this wind is a mixed blessing.

As night falls we pick out the light at the entrance to the northwest channel into Key West. In these pre-GPS days, making a night entry into a strange harbor beset with reefs and with strong following winds and seas is a nail-biting, stomach-churning affair. Instinct and caution dictate that we hold off, heave-to for the night, and enter at dawn, but there are few things more devastating to the morale of a seasick sailor than to be rolling around all night in sight of a safe haven. I badly want to get Terrie and Pippin ashore and end this voyage.

HEAVING-TO

Heaving-to is the traditional response to heavy weather. By the time it becomes necessary, there are generally a couple of reefs in the main, and the headsail (jib) is also well reefed. In the case of a cutter, the jib or genoa will have been taken down or furled, to be replaced by the staysail, which may in its turn be reefed. If the boat has a trysail (a tiny storm sail), it may have been set in place of the reefed main. On a ketch, the mainsail may have been stowed and the mizzen sail set.

With this kind of a sailplan, in principle heaving-to is simplicity itself. The boat is tacked but without releasing the jib or staysail sheet. On the new tack, the mainsail (or trysail or mizzen) will be driving the boat up to windward, while the backed jib or staysail will be knocking the bow off the wind. The idea is to establish a balance in which the boat lies about 45 degrees to 50 degrees off the wind, making minimal forward motion and not much leeway. On traditional, long-keeled boats such as *Nada* the desired effect will almost always be achieved by lashing the tiller to leeward, or the wheel to windward, so that the rudder is turning the boat into the wind. On modern fin-keeled boats it may not be possible to get the boat to hold a consistent angle to the wind, in which case heaving-to will not work. Note that on no account should a boat be heaved-to with an overlapping headsail—it will soon be torn to pieces on the spreaders.

If a boat can be made to heave-to reliably, it is quite amazing the difference it makes to onboard comfort. A boat that moments before was crashing into and off waves will settle down into gently bucking and rolling. Down below, with the noise of the gale outside muted, the crew can relax and rest while they wait for the gale to blow itself out. Many cruisers on a rough passage will heave-to from time to time, even when not strictly necessary just to have a meal in peace or to get a little rest.

A break in the clouds with a full moon shining through gives us a chance to feel our way into the channel, one eye on the depthsounder, the other on the loran (the forerunner of GPS), which is performing faultlessly, albeit off to the southeast by approximately a quarter of a mile, a quantity which we easily establish at the sea buoy. Once inside the outer jetties the seas subside and we have no problems in the well-lit channel. That same night a 40-foot ketch, similar to ours, is lost to the east. The skipper mistook a reef marker for a channel marker and drove his boat onto the rocks.

Monday morning 0130 finds us tied to the dock in Key West, 5 days and 15 minutes out of Mandeville. Street artists, fire-eaters, and clowns greet us, having congregated for an international buskers festival. It is one of the strange quirks of seasickness that once it is over it is almost immediately forgotten. Terrie and Pippin perk up. On the dock Pippin is a comical sight, rolling around on her sea legs like a drunken sailor.

By the following night the boat is cleaned, the discomforts of the voyage behind us. My log reads: "Terrie has bounced right back and is ready to go on again." In the evening the local gaff-rigged schooners are silhouetted in a stately parade by an orange sun as it sinks into the sea. We bid Ray and Lyle farewell as they leave, returning to home and work. The carefree atmosphere of Key West eases away the tensions of years of hard labor and an unpleasant crossing.

* * * * *

We find Key West still suspended in hippy days. It is a riotous clapboard town, larger than life; the old stomping ground of Ernest Hemingway; a home for many a 60s misfit and would-be buccaneer; the songs of Jimmy Buffett brought to life; and the last stopping place in the continental U.S. before the final flight to the "islands". We linger for days.

In an old warehouse we gaze in awe at piles of silver ingots, stacked like bricks on a building site. Sacks spill gold and silver coins through rotten fabric; there are fabulous gold chains and jewelry and some of the finest emeralds in the world. This is just part of the forty tons of treasure still being recovered by Indiana-born chicken farmer Mel Fisher from the wreck of the *Atocha,* a magnificent Spanish galleon. A film chronicles Fisher's sixteen-year obsessive quest for treasure, during which he lost his eldest son and two others.

Between trips ashore I work on the boat fixing the minor breakdowns while Terrie extends the lee cloth on one of the berths, converting it into a padded cell so that Pippin can be safely contained at sea if both of us need to work the boat.

The failure of the autopilot is particularly disconcerting and by far my biggest problem. It is clear with Terrie becoming increasingly large with child and Pippin requiring almost constant attention when at sea that we are going to have to singlehand the boat much of the time. For this we need help at the helm.

The bearings on the autopilot actuator, the arm that moves in and out to turn the tiller, have been destroyed by excessive steering loads. I have to reduce these loads but can see no way to do so until I realize the answer is staring me in the face. We have a homebuilt windvane self-steering device that controls *Nada*'s rudder via a trim tab mounted on the rudder's trailing edge. The trim

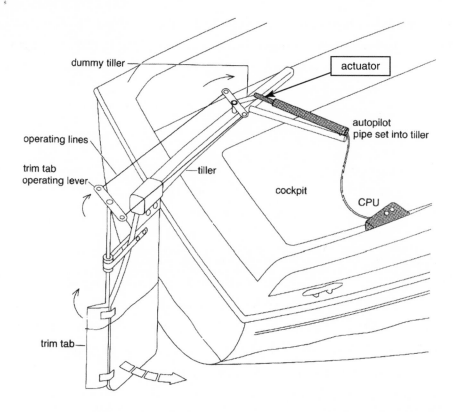

dummy tiller

actuator

autopilot
pipe set into tiller

operating lines

trim tab
operating lever

tiller

cockpit

CPU

trim tab

tab is extremely effective, but the windvane part of the rig has never worked too well and as such sees little use. All I have to do is connect the autopilot to the trim tab, using the leverage the trim tab exerts on the rudder to steer the boat. The autopilot loads will now be minimal.

The engineering takes a bit of thought but in a couple of days the job is done. A new mini-tiller mounted to the top of the main tiller operates the trim tab via a couple of cables. A pipe fastened into the main tiller at right angles to it holds the autopilot actuator, which is clipped onto the mini-tiller. A quick-release pin disconnects the autopilot when the windvane is in use. The rig is strong, simple, and easy to set up and take down.

Everything needed for the new installation has come out of onboard stores: stainless steel plate and pipe; a bench vise, hacksaw, drill and bits; files, taps, and dies; bolts and screws; wood, glue, and varnish; cable and end fittings. No wonder poor *Nada* is sitting so low in the water. We simply have to do something about this: Terrie and I are beginning to argue daily over cutting back on supplies, tidying up the boat, reducing weight, and making *Nada* easier to sail and keep organized.

I start making a list of things to go. This provokes a row. "Terrie, we have got to get rid of some of this junk." "It's not my stuff that weighs so much; it's all your damn tools and that stupid stove..." A low blow, this one. The stove in question is a heavy old Dickinson diesel with a cast iron top that turns the whole boat into an oven in the tropics. I bought it based on a glowing recommendation in one of Hal Roth's books (see Further Reading, page 187), failing to note that he was sailing in the cold Pacific Northwest. I have built into it a water heater coil attached to a 7-gallon hot water tank set high on the cabin side. The two together give the boat a permanent list to starboard. The stove has been a big, heavy, expensive mistake.

The next day Terrie goes grocery shopping. When she comes back the stove, water tank, and associated plumbing are ripped out of the boat and sitting on the dock. "Now what are you going to throw out, Terrie?" "You're crazy. What are we going to cook on?" Slowly we argue our way to some semblance of a compromise and tempers cool but that leaves us with the question: what are we going to cook on? Clearly we need another, lighter stove and the best place to find one is Fort Lauderdale. We have to move in any case: the dockage fees at Key West are way beyond our budget.

* * * * *

Between the Florida Keys and Cuba the Gulf Stream pours out of the Gulf of Mexico and hooks around in a wide arc to sweep up the Florida coastline at speeds of up to 4 knots. We head out to sea that evening, just the three of us for the first time, to catch the Stream, fouling a crab pot on the way that fortunately we are able to knock loose. Through the night we beat to windward to clear the Keys and then slowly ease the sheets as we pick up the Stream and come around onto a more northerly course. By the following morning we are running almost dead downwind, our round bilge boat rolling heavily in the Gulf Stream swells, dipping first one rail and then the other in the water. It is a major effort to move about on the boat, almost impossible to sleep in spite of lee cloths, and Pippin is unsafe on her own and has to be held all the time. The new autopilot rig works like a charm, which is just as well since we are all three of us seasick at one time or another.

We enter the Intracoastal Waterway (ICW) at Fort Lauderdale shortly before dusk and turn north toward the anchorage at Las Olas Boulevard. Ahead is a red channel marker. Automatically, I steer to pass it to starboard (following the U.S. *Red Right Returning* rule, which is the opposite of the rest of the world) and promptly run aground—I have forgotten that the waterway has a different set of navigational rules than those that guide vessels in the open sea. I put *Nada* hard in reverse while Terrie deposits Pippin in her "cell" and then the two of us rush from side to side together. Passing powerboaters probably think we have lost our minds, but by coordinating the rate at which we move with the rate *Nada* rolls we are able to reinforce the roll until the grip of the mud on *Nada*'s keel is broken and we pull free.

We motor the short distance to Las Olas Boulevard. The anchorage is crowded with inadequate swinging room for late arrivals such as ourselves but it is now dark and we have nowhere else to go. We move into a moderately open space and, at the second attempt, get the anchor to hold on short scope. Later that night the wind and tide turn, swinging us uncomfortably close to another boat. At 0130 we haul up the anchor and move onto a vacant dock for the remainder of the night, only to be chased off in the morning by the police. Fortunately, by this time one or two boats have left and we find adequate swinging room in the anchorage.

ANCHORING ROUTINES

Over the course of our shakedown cruise, Terrie and I evolved an anchoring routine that has worked well for us ever since. It goes something like this:

- On the approach to an anchorage we crank the engine and lower or furl the sails, but leave them ready to hoist in case of engine failure.

- If the dinghy is being towed, we shorten the painter to the point that we cannot suck it into the propeller when going into reverse.

- We make a pass through the anchorage, looking for a likely spot to drop the anchor, and then, if the depths are at all in doubt, circle slowly around, checking the depths at the limit of our projected swinging circle to make sure that there are no unpleasant surprises.

- While circling, we look at how any other boats are lying (to the wind, or to a tidal stream or current, or maybe a bit of both) and attempt to gauge their likely turning circles. The hardest situation to gauge is one in which the wind is blowing against the tide. Anchored boats may all be lined up with the wind, making you think that their rodes are stretched out in front of them, whereas the current may have carried the boats up wind so that the rodes are in fact streaming aft. In such a situation, it is common to misjudge the point at which to drop your anchor. Only after it is down will it become apparent that it is in the wrong place! It will have to be retrieved and reset.

- Terrie and I have an agreed set of hand signals for communicating so that we do not need to shout to one another. We point to port or starboard to indicate a turn, forward to come on, and backward to reverse. We wiggle a forefinger in the air to indicate speed up, and wiggle it down toward the deck to indicate slow down. We put a hand up for neutral and across our throat to shut the engine down.

- Having picked a likely spot, we approach slowly upwind (or current, if this is having a greater impact on nearby boats). The chain is eased out to get the anchor hanging down so that it will be easy to launch. In a crowded anchorage we come pretty much under the stern of the boat behind which we intend to anchor. We will fall back from here once the anchor is down.

- When we are over the chosen spot (sometimes nowadays we will mark this on our electronic charts), we stop *Nada* and the signal is given to launch the anchor. The windlass clutch is let loose.
- We lower the anchor to the bottom with just enough rode to get it there. We either back down *slowly*, or else sit in neutral and allow the wind to blow the boat's head off, as we continue to pay out rode *at the same rate as the boat reverses or drifts*. This ensures that there will be no pile up on the bottom that might foul the anchor. If we are allowing the wind to blow us off, the boat's head will come around broadside to the wind, and the boat will take off at a tangent. It may also be doing the same in reverse. This is normal.
- With chain, when we have about 3:1 scope out, and with nylon at around 5:1, we *gently* snub up on the rode, using the clutch on the windlass for the chain, or the warping drum or a cleat for nylon. The idea is to ease the anchor's flukes into the bottom as the rode continues to pay out, now under a little tension, and then to fully snub up.
- We will then often stop for a cup of tea, especially in doubtful bottoms (such as the thin sand over rock found in many Caribbean anchorages, or thick weed and kelp found in other parts of the world) before fully loading the anchor. This gives the anchor additional time to work its flukes into the bottom. Finally, we gradually increase the speed in reverse to something over ⅔ rds the rated engine speed to thoroughly dig in the anchor and test its set. While this is going on we keep a hand or bare foot on the rode.
- If the anchor is dragging the rode will alternately tighten and slacken; if it is dragging on rocks or some other hard bottom, it will transmit irregular vibrations up the rode. At the first sign of dragging we go into neutral, pay out a slug of rode (maybe 10 or 15 feet) and then gently snub up once again in hopes of teasing the anchor into the bottom. If this fails, and if we have lots of

dragging room, we may continue to pull the anchor around for a while, paying out some more rode as we go, to see if it will take a bite. If room is restricted, we go ahead, recover the anchor and we start again, but not before bringing the anchor to the surface to make sure that its flukes are not fouled. In warm shallowish water, if repeated attempts fail to set the anchor, we snorkel down and do it by hand. We often check the set in Caribbean anchorages the same way.

- Assuming the anchor takes a hold, we check the set by finding a range (for example, the mast of another boat in line with a tree ashore, or a house in line with a tree) and watch this while maintaining the engine speed. If the two objects remain in line, the set is good.
- If we are lying to a chain rode, I now put on a nylon snubber, pay out some chain, and take a turn with the loose chain around a cleat in case the snubber breaks. If we are lying to a nylon rode, if appropriate I add chafing gear at the bow roller.
- If this is not an officially designated anchorage, it may be necessary to hoist into the rigging an appropriate anchoring daymark (the COLREGS require a black ball; this rule is almost never enforced in the Americas, but frequently is in Europe).

The same procedure can be used by a singlehander except that it might prove useful to run the anchor rode through the bow roller, bring it back over the lifelines, attach the anchor, and then haul the anchor aft (outside of all rigging) to the cockpit so that it can be launched from the cockpit.

SETTING MORE THAN ONE ANCHOR

It is not uncommon to set two anchors. Good reasons are:

- Because the holding is poor;
- Because a big blow is expected;

- To hold the boat off a hazard if the wind shifts;
- To keep the boat more-or-less in one spot;
- To hold the boat into a chop in a wind over tide situation; or
- Simply for peace of mind at night.

Where the holding is poor, or a big blow is expected, the anchors should be set fairly close to one another. I like to place them about 30 degrees apart. The first is set in the usual fashion, and then the boat is motored forward at the appropriate angle until alongside the first anchor, at which point the second is let go. This is easier said than done, since it is very hard to judge just where that first anchor is! If you go too far you risk dislodging the first from its set, and if you don't go far enough you end up with too little scope on the second.

I like to use a rope rode on the first anchor (with a length of chain at the anchor), and our chain (primary) rode on the second anchor. As we motor forward to drop the second anchor, I leave the first rode cleated off but pull in the slack by hand and let it pile up on deck, maintaining a little tension on the line. At some point, the rode stops coming in and I have to start letting it out again. I know now that I am more-or-less alongside the first anchor. What is more, by maintaining a little tension on the first rode while motoring forward, I ensure that we do not foul it in the propeller.

We keep going forward a little more, letting out the rode to the first anchor, to give ourselves some dragging room with the second anchor, and then come to a stop and drop the second anchor. As we fall back, I let the rode to the first anchor run back out, snubbing up the second anchor before the first rode comes taut. This way I can ensure that the second anchor is also well set.

It may be that we are anchored off a beach close enough inshore that if the wind shifts we are going to end up on the beach. In this case, the second anchor will be set in such a way as to hold us off the beach if necessary. This may be well out to one side, or it may be dead astern.

Fort Lauderdale is the home of Sailorman, the best secondhand boat store in the U.S. We dinghy ashore, hire a rental car, load up our old stove, water tank, 300 feet of ¾-inch nylon braid, and various other bits and pieces, and drive over. Already *Nada* is several hundred pounds lighter.

Although for good reason propane stoves predominate on boats, and contemporary installation standards ensure their safety, when on the oilrigs I was seriously burned in a natural gas fire; I am fearful of having any form of gas on the boat and want some kind of liquid fuel. We hunt through the shelves at Sailorman and find an old Blakes two-burner kerosene stove with a small oven; I buy it, ignoring the fact that it is probably there because someone got frustrated with it and converted to propane! Two days later the stove is plumbed in, everything is stowed neatly, and we are ready to go. Years later our Dickinson stove was still high on a shelf at Sailorman and for all I know is still there, while the kerosene stove eventually gave us a lot of trouble. I finally conquered my fears and converted to propane.

While in Fort Lauderdale we make one other purchase that severely dents the cruising kitty—a satnav, a first-generation satellite navigation system. With it installed, we pull out our charts for the Bahamas and the West Indies. We are about to go cruising.

FROM *NADA I* TO *NADA IV*

In the late 1800s Colin Archer, a Norwegian naval architect and boatbuilder, created a 47-foot sailing rescue boat (the Redningskoite) whose mission was to stand by at sea with the Norwegian fishing fleets in the worst possible conditions and rescue fishermen as necessary. The double-ended design became synonymous with seaworthiness. In 1925 William Atkin scaled it down to the 32-foot *Eric* ketch. Vito Dumas made one of the first solo circumnavigations in a boat of this design, but what really put it on the map was when Robin Knox-Johnston won the first non-stop singlehanded race around the world in his *Suhaili*. In the 1970s the design was adapted into kit form by William Crealock as the

Westsail 32, the boat at the center of Ferenc Maté's *From a Bare Hull*. Hundreds were built.

In 1934 William Atkin drew the 38-foot Ingrid as another scaled-down version of Colin Archer's famous design. The Ingrid featured in Maté's book as the perfect cruising boat. It was this that seduced me away from the Bruce Robert's 38-foot plans we were about to purchase.

The defining features of the Archer design and their derivatives are a relatively narrow beam with a rounded (double-ended) stern, a full keel, and heavy displacement. About the time we were building our *Nada*, Bruce Farr, a young New Zealand naval architect, and his partner Russell Bowler, were cleaning up on the race course sailing lightweight, broad-beamed, fin-keeled boats with ever increasingly wide transoms. Wins in their boats included several round-the-world races. It took a while for the message to get through, but eventually the cruising community came to realize that you could have seaworthiness without pinched sterns (and the resulting loss of interior space), long keels, and heavy displacement.

After 10 years of cruising mostly around the Caribbean and the Gulf of Mexico I sold our *Nada* (over the strong objections of Terrie and the children, who were now old enough to express an opinion and were sentimentally attached to *Nada*) and replaced her with *Nada II*, a Pacific Seacraft 40. The Pacific Seacraft was in all respects a compromise between old and new. The long keel was foreshortened, the double-ended stern converted to a canoe stern (which carries the beam farther aft), and the weight reduced. *Nada II* was just as seaworthy and comfortable as *Nada* and performed considerably better on all points of sail. After a six-month cruise around the northwest Caribbean, I happened to overhear Terrie talking on the phone with one of her girlfriends who, knowing how pissed off Terrie had been with me for selling *Nada*, asked her, "Do you miss the old boat?" Terrie replied, "Not one bit." So I guess I got that one right.

After five years sailing *Nada II*, she was replaced by *Nada*s *III* and *IV*—a Malo 45 and 46, to all intents and purposes the same boat but with different mechanical and electrical systems based on hybrid and other experiments we have been conducting. The Malos have a shorter keel still and transom sterns, which really opens up the interior space aft. They are just as seaworthy as, and more comfortable than, our previous *Nada*s. Performance is once again enhanced on all points of sail. However, although I needed the extra volume for the equipment involved in our various test programs, Terrie has never been comfortable with such large boats, primarily because they give the impression we must be rich. I thought she'd come to appreciate the improved performance and added comfort but she has, to date, not stopped bugging me to get a smaller boat. I guess I got that one wrong.

By contemporary standards, *Nada*s *III* and *IV* are still very conservative. I have, on occasion, considered much higher performing boats, but given our propensity to seasickness and Terrie's lack of interest in sailing even after all these years, I opted for comfort and security. These are boats that have taken care of us through gales and pretty awful conditions, and that have the capacity to carry the equipment necessary for a high standard of living in far-off anchorages. If I were to build another boat today, if I could change anything, it would only be Terrie's opinion!

NADA'S PROPENSITY TO HEEL—STABILITY 101

Single-hulled sailboats such as *Nada* (as opposed to catamarans and trimarans) all have a ballast keel of some sort protruding beneath the boat. When the boat is upright, this defines the maximum draft of the boat. As a boat heels, the ballast at the end of the keel acts as a lever arm to counteract the heeling. The greater the heeling, the more the lever arm moves up until, and even beyond, the point at which the boat is lying on its side. As the boat heels, the keel increasingly angles away from the bottom, reducing the draft.

The beamier the boat and the more the interior volume at its ends, together with a sharper angle between the sides and bottom of the hull, the greater the buoyancy, and the harder it is to heel the boat over, with or without a ballast keel; when sailing to windward there is always some initial heeling, but this will be limited. (This is known as initial stability.) At the other extreme we have the Ingrid design, with a combination of a narrow beam, a double-ended stern with little volume, and rounded cross-sections: the net effect is little initial stability. When going to windward, Ingrids are easily heeled by 10–20 degrees, after which the ballast kicks in to counteract further heeling.

In the case of our *Nada*, we overbuilt the deck, adding weight high up that further reduced her initial stability, and unknowingly under-ballasted her with 7,700 lbs. of lead (which was what was recommended by the builder from whom we bought our hull) as opposed to the 10,000 called for in William Atkin's original 1930s design. *Nada* was excessively tender and easily heeled well beyond 20 degrees, and sometimes 30 degrees. We could not go to windward in anything more than a light breeze without putting the caprail, and often the entire side deck, underwater.

There was a hidden benefit here—if we ran hard aground we could set an anchor off to one or other side, attach either a mainsail or headsail halyard to the anchor, and crank on the halyard so that the pull on the anchor was now from the masthead. The lever arm created by the mast enabled us to relatively easily roll *Nada* over until her 6-foot draft was reduced to not much over 4 feet. Over the years during our numerous explorations of poorly charted regions in *Nada* we ran aground many times. On a number of occasions we dragged ourselves off, or were dragged off by other boats, by pulling from the masthead (see page 13).

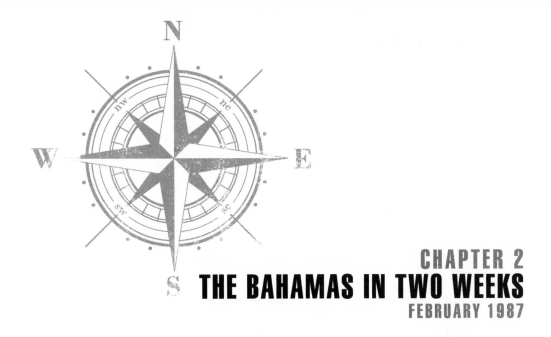

CHAPTER 2
THE BAHAMAS IN TWO WEEKS
FEBRUARY 1987

RAY DECIDES TO REJOIN us for the crossing of the Gulf Stream to Nassau. He flies into Miami while we wait for him with our rental car at Fort Lauderdale airport; in these pre cell-phone days it takes a while to sort that out. We are learning a new lesson which is to be repeatedly reinforced (but which takes us another twenty-five years to fully act upon!): much though friends and relatives might dream of sailing with us for a week or two, and much though we might look forward to their company, it is hard to correlate a cruising lifestyle with rendezvous points and other people's work schedules.

Airline tickets are generally booked weeks in advance. How can we know where we will be? We may find some particularly alluring island and stop for a month. In any event, a boat's movements are determined by weather patterns measured in days and weeks, not airline schedules timed to the nearest minute. And once the rendezvous is made, what if the visitors have only a week to travel to their departure point on another island and the boat is storm bound in harbor all week?

Once we have Ray on board our immediate destination is Nassau. Our charts of the Bahamas—the only ones available in 1987—are based on surveys from the 1830s. There are no details for the shallow banks that cover much

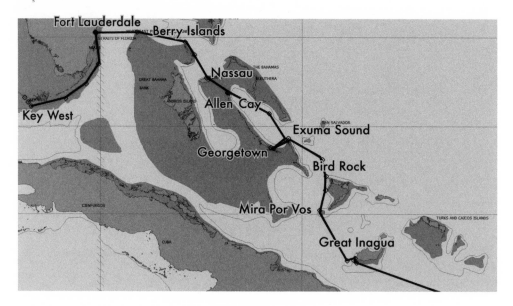

of the Bahamas, and in particular for the banks between the Bimini Islands, southeast of Fort Lauderdale, and Nassau. (These details were not filled in until years later, largely due to the painstaking and accurate pioneering work of Monty and Sarah Lewis at Explorer Charts.) We incorrectly assume we have to pass to the north of the Biminis, rounding the Great Isaac Lighthouse, which will bring us into the deep water of the Northwest Providence Channel and take us to the north of the Berry Islands. A turn to the southeast will then bring us to Nassau.

Ray brings with him another cold front with strong winds from the northwest. I am keen to set sail and ride this wind, fearful that as the front passes the wind will veer into the east and put us on a hard beat to Nassau after rounding the Berry Islands. But other sailors unnerve us with tales of 25-foot square-sided waves thrown up when a nor'wester blows against the Gulf Stream. We delay a few precious hours and go grocery shopping; it is to cost us dear.

When we finally get under way we have a marvelous night run across the Gulf Stream, steering just south of east, allowing the powerful stream to set us north to clear the Great Isaac light. Under jib and main we run at well over hull speed, fighting the tendency to round up and broach as each 8- to 10-foot sea comes barreling up on the stern quarter and whooshes by. This is sailing at its most exhilarating, a reminder of just how much fun it can be. But by the time we round Great Isaac the wind is already veering into the north, and then the northeast. We progressively harden the sheets as we passage the Northwest Providence Channel. Soon we are beating up to Great Stirrup Cay, the northernmost of the Berry Islands, and then we can no longer hold the course and are steadily set to the southeast, finally having to tack and work our way around to the north of the Berry Islands, hard on the wind, side decks periodically awash, mother and baby looking increasingly miserable.

If we had left Fort Lauderdale just four hours earlier we would have rounded Great Stirrup on a reach in comfort and style some 6 hours ahead of the time it eventually takes us to beat around. And then as the wind veered we would still have been able to reach all the way southeast to Nassau. If, if, if. As it is, by the time we round the Berrys the wind is already in the east and we have a wet and uncomfortable beat all the way to Nassau, set to the west and having to tack back up. We learn another lesson: there tends to be a form of "groupthink" that magnifies the challenges and raises unnecessary fears when cruisers congregate ahead of a passage; you need to have faith in your boat and judgment and don't be deterred by others!

Through the evening hours our open cockpit is repeatedly drenched in spray. The rail is under much of the time and the larger waves come surging up the side deck to break over the cockpit coaming. Soon after midnight an alarmed Terrie scrambles out of the cabin, where she has been holding a fractious Pippin, to tell us water and oil are running over the cabin sole. I dive inside. It is coming from the engine room. I have left a vent, set into the cockpit coaming, open. Water making its way below has flooded the engine drip pan and finally washed the oil into the cabin. What a terrible slippery mess it has made. It is amazing how far a little dirty oil can go.

We raise the Nassau light on Paradise Island in the early hours of the morning and are once again faced with the choice of heaving-to until daylight or entering a strange harbor at night. This time I have no qualms: Nassau is a great big, wide open, well lit, roadstead between Paradise Island and New Providence Island. What could go wrong?

We crank the motor and head in. As we close the harbor we become more and more disoriented. Nothing seems to fit our three-year-old chart. I am red/green color blind and think maybe my eyes are playing tricks on me, but neither Ray nor Terrie can come up with any of the lights shown on the chart.

We are now close enough to see the lights of cruise ships anchored in the harbor, beckoning us in. We ease on toward the Nassau light, which our chart indicates is on the tip of Paradise Island, confident that at least there are no dangers between us and the island, and wondering if we are simply unable to pick out the various channel lights against the confusing backdrop of lights from the city. Suddenly a massive breakwater looms out of the darkness dead ahead, a frightening sight. In panic we tack just before we hit. Considerably shaken, we motor out to sea and heave-to until dawn. We pore over the charts completely baffled, looking for an explanation and finding none.

With dawn's early light all becomes clear: the red 9-mile light on the west breakwater is out; the green 9-mile light on the east breakwater is out; the two flashing red channel markers are out; and the Paradise Island light, the oldest lighthouse in the West Indies, built in 1817, is out. We have mistaken a light on the other side of the harbor for the Paradise Island light; we almost ran up on the west breakwater. We sail in and drop our 45 lb. CQR anchor below the Paradise Island bridge.

The holding is awful. We have to set the anchor seven times, pulling it up laboriously with our hand-cranked windlass between each attempt, before it takes even a halfway decent bite on the bottom. I am reasonably certain that if I back down hard on the anchor to check its set, as I normally do, it will drag again so instead I ease off on the throttle and motor forward to drop a second anchor as a backup.

Nassau is far from a cruiser's delight. The town is over-priced and over-run with tourists; theft is rampant and foreigners are mostly seen as an easy way to make a buck. We have no desire to stay but are held in harbor as another powerful norther passes through with 25- to 30-knot winds.

A trimaran dragging out of control through the anchorage cuts loose from three anchors while we spend a sleepless night nervously eyeing adjacent boats, checking our rodes, and wishing we had done a better job of setting our anchors. In the morning Pippin puts her hand in the priming flame for the new kerosene oven and seriously burns two fingers. This cruising life is not quite as we had imagined it! Ray returns home. As soon as the wind eases, we take the opportunity to head south.

* * * * *

The Bahamas encompass around 750,000 square miles, most of it water, of which almost half consists of shallow banks over which the depths rarely exceed 30 feet and are commonly much less. The banks are liberally sprinkled with coral heads and shoal areas that rise to within a foot or two of the surface. In many places the banks are rimmed by small islands, on the other side of which, and along the open edges of the banks, the bottom drops away precipitously to depths of thousands of feet. Although there is little change in depth with the tides, the vast area of the banks together with the narrow passages between some of the islands can result in powerful currents with standing waves (which the Bahamaians call a "rage") when the wind is blowing against the tide.

The banks have never been systematically surveyed by any official hydrographic office and to this day the International Hydrographic Office classifies 100% of Bahamian waters as needing resurvey. By the time of our arrival in 1987 one or two adventurous cruising sailors have defined a number of viable routes across the banks and described these in early cruising guides but no one has developed reliable charts (as mentioned earlier, these only came much later with the work of Monty and Sarah Lewis). Our onward passage from Nassau will take us across the White and Yellow Banks, where our charts are effectively useless. We will be following one of the routes in the guides.

The day we leave it seems as if half the boats in the harbor have the same idea. At the Porgee light—east of Nassau, where the various routes across the shallow banks diverge—there are scattered sails in every direction as far

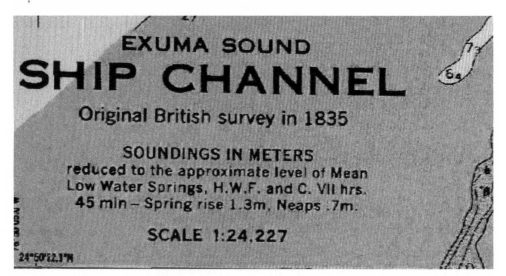

as the eye can see. It is a glorious day with clear skies and a light breeze: fine conditions in which to get our first taste of banks sailing as we make for Allen Cay some forty miles away.

We take a bearing on the Porgee Rocks light with a hand bearing compass and head south-southeast, piloting on dead reckoning and rather imprecise fixes on the tips of New Providence and Rose Islands. We have to allow for a substantial tide setting on and off the banks, but at all times there are little pieces of floating grass and other debris that provide an indication of the tidal speed and direction over the bottom, which, thankfully, is always visible.

Navigating on the banks is strictly a daytime affair. Water depths rarely exceed 15 feet and are frequently less than ten; heavily laden as we are, our draft is just a little over 6 feet. Coral heads thrust up to within feet of the surface. The water is crystal clear, the bottom alternating patches of sand with weeds and coral. The color of the water is all-important: the more intense the blue, the deeper the water. White areas denote shoals with sandy bottoms; brown, weed or coral heads. It is best to sail with the sun above and behind the boat as this eliminates glare and illuminates the bottom. It takes a little getting used to.

NAVIGATING IN CORAL

Navigating in coral poses special challenges (and delights) all its own.

Coral reefs frequently sit atop plateaus that emerge quite suddenly from great depths (and so will not be detected by a depthsounder until the boat is almost on the reef) and that have very little, or no, land mass above sea level (so little, or nothing, is visible above the horizon). When you add to this the fact that many coral-strewn waters are poorly charted, you can see why so many boats are lost on reefs in the Caribbean and especially the Pacific.

When approaching a reef for the first time, it is essential to place no reliance on electronic navigation, to make any approach in good light, and to maintain a bow watch as the region of the reef is approached. Once in the vicinity of a reef piloting is mostly an eyeball affair.

Coral will not grow where sediment is present, so almost always the water around reefs is clear, sometimes astonishingly clear. In the right light conditions, this makes it easy to pick out coral patches and reefs, but in the wrong light conditions nothing will be seen. "Right" light means with the sun well above the horizon, and preferably behind the boat or overhead, but certainly not ahead (this will create a glare that will obscure visibility). There are then two key ingredients to picking a path through coral: a perch as high as possible on the boat (standing on the bow pulpit may be the best you can do, but ideally there will be ratlines or mast steps to the lower spreaders) and a high quality pair of polarized sunglasses. The latter are absolutely essential.

With polarized sunglasses it doesn't take long to get your eye "tuned in". Pretty soon you will be able to distinguish sand bottoms from turtle grass and coral, and estimate with a surprising degree of accuracy (down to inches) the depth of the water. That is, so long as the sun is still in the right position and not obscured by clouds. The minute the sun becomes obscured you will find it next-to-impossible to pick out coral, even if it is almost breaking the surface of the water. It is time to anchor and wait for better conditions.

What this means is that when picking your way through a substantial amount of coral you need to make sure the sky is clear and that you will have adequate light conditions to see you through to a safe anchorage. You should also have in mind secure locations to hole up if conditions unexpectedly deteriorate. Over the years we have more than once been forced to anchor for the night in the midst of a veritable coral maze because we ran out of the necessary light conditions to finish picking our way through.

The first few hours we are extremely tense, running to the bowsprit, up the ratlines which we have installed between our lower shrouds, back to the bowsprit. Wherever the depths appear to be critical, or the coral menacing, one of us climbs up the ratlines and onto the lower spreaders from whence a good view of the surrounding seabed is gained. We mistake weed at navigable depths for jutting coral, and dodge more than one shadow of a small cloud. However, things quickly fall into place; by mid-afternoon we are laid back in the cockpit making laconic ascents to the spreaders from time to time, Mr. Autohelm at the tiller.

At noon I had pulled out the sextant and taken a routine LAN (Local Apparent Noon) sight but otherwise the sextant stays in its box. By now we are alone, our heavy cruising boat falling behind the rest of the pack in the light variable airs. As the afternoon wears on I crank the motor, unwilling to work into the unknown Allen Cay after dark. We have already found the Loran to be highly inaccurate in the Bahamas so I turn on the satnav (which, to limit its energy drain, I only use as and when needed).

At dusk we close a series of islands, unsure of our position but not in the least bit concerned—the satnav will provide an accurate fix. It gives us a fix some 50 miles off my dead reckoning. That quickly shakes me out of my complacency. I am very much regretting that I haven't taken at least one afternoon sextant sight; it isn't as if I have been doing anything other than lazing around working on a tan. We have only a short time to make an anchorage before dark and the last thing I want to do is spend the night on the Banks among the coral heads.

Landfalls in the Bahamas are not easy. The majority of islands are low-lying and covered with scrubby vegetation—not very interesting in fact: the real glories of the Bahamas lie underwater. Few islands are visible from the deck of a sailboat at more than five miles and one looks very much like another. We close a string of islands anxiously consulting our cruising guide and debating whether this or that hump is the one illustrated in the book. In the end we find we are just a mile or so north of our intended track and are safely tucked into Allen Cay in the company of a dozen other boats as night falls.

The following morning the wind is in the northeast on another perfect day. The clear water around Allen Cay looks oh so inviting, and we have yet to wet our snorkeling gear, but we are loathe to pass up this favorable wind. Reluctantly, we decide to make all speed south for as long as we can. We pick our way through the coral and out the other side of the anchorage into Exuma Sound. In thirty minutes we are making 6 knots in 700 fathoms with 2- to 4-foot seas—what a dramatic contrast from one side of an island to another. One day we are in 10 feet of water dodging coral heads, the next in 4,000 feet.

The Exumas run more or less northwest to southeast, some 120 miles long. Farther southeast lies Long Island; to the east Cat Island. We need to round Cape Santa Maria on the northern tip of Long Island. It seems likely the wind will follow its typical post-cold-front pattern, veering to the east and then the southeast, so we make up toward the east; this will give us room to come around with the wind and still clear Cape Santa Maria.

Throughout the day the wind builds and works its way into the east and then south of east. From broad reaching under all sail we are slowly reduced to close-hauled under jib and mizzen. And then we can no longer hold the course but have made sufficient easting to still have hopes of rounding Long Island.

During the night we raise the light on Cape Santa Maria but then we are headed altogether by the shifting wind and faced with an arduous beat to windward to round the Cape. Frustration: here we are on top of our objective but unable to fetch it. Even if we do work our way around, our next planned destination, the Turks and Caicos islands, are now many miles upwind.

We are learning the hard way the disadvantages of our overbuilt, heavy displacement, long-keeled boat as compared to a more modern design that would take the windward work in stride. In the early hours of the morning we bear away for George Town on Great Exuma Island, which lies downwind. After having pushed to make all speed possible we now drop the mizzen to slow down and avoid coming into George Town's Elizabeth Harbour in the dark.

With the dawn the coastline comes up over the horizon. We crank the motor and check the satnav to confirm my dead reckoning. Yet another improbable fix after the beast has given us faultless fixes periodically through the night. We work our way through the fringing reef into the southern end of Elizabeth Harbour using Kline's *Yachtsman's Guide to the Bahamas* and anchor in the sheltered water behind Stocking Island.

We are tired. We spend the day doing minor chores and repairs around the boat, planning to go sightseeing in George Town the next day after a good night's sleep. We have heard numerous favorable reports about the town and are excited at the prospect of exploring ashore. But during the night the wind begins to veer. The following morning we pick up a forecast of a fresh cold front coming through, packing northwest winds of 25 knots; this should give us a couple of days of favorable winds, enough to blow us to the Turks and Caicos, approximately 250 miles to the southeast. While the other boats set about finding more sheltered water or doubling up on their anchors, soon after midday we pull ours up and make for the open sea. We have not set foot on land.

In just a few hours we round Cape Santa Maria and are running before the wind at 6 to 7 knots under a single poled-out jib. Once again we make up to the east anticipating a wind shift after the front goes through. Unfortunately this occurs much sooner than expected, with the wind steadily veering toward the southeast. We are gradually forced to crank in the sheets until we are close-hauled, beating to round Bird Rock on the northern tip of Crooked Island. In

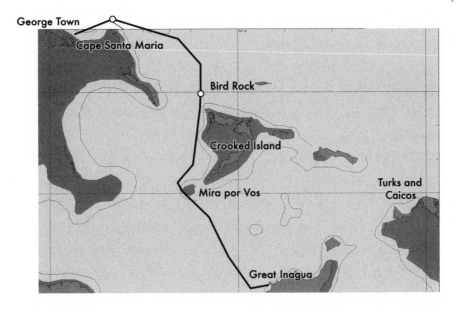

the early hours of the morning we sight the loom of Bird Rock light, and then can no longer hold a course to round it. The Turks and Caicos even now are still miles to windward. With a distinct feeling of deja vu we bear away and set course for Great Inagua Island to the south, passing Bird Rock at dawn.

The Crooked Island-Acklins-Long Cay archipelago forms a large crescent, curving away to the east and then hooking back to the west. At its southern end a 7-mile wide channel passes between Castle Island and the aptly named Mira por Vos Shoals (Look Out for Yourself!). Throughout the day we run almost due south, sighting land in mid-afternoon that we take to be Castle Island. The satnav chooses this part of the day to reject every fix.

With cloud cover all afternoon I have taken no sextant sights. No matter, it is straightforward enough. We harden up the sheets somewhat in order to close Castle Island for a positive fix but as we approach something seems wrong. It finally dawns on me that instead of looking at a 60-foot hill some 5 or 6 miles off I am looking at a 20-foot Limestone Cay less than 2 miles off—an interesting demonstration of our powers of self-deception when we are convinced we know what we are seeing. We have been set 8 miles to the west in a matter of hours by a tidal stream flowing off the Crooked Islands and are sailing directly for the Mira por Vos Shoals. My log reads: "Should have known better from tracks of ships."

Forced to pass to the west of the Cays we are once again close-hauled in order to make Great Inagua, the southernmost island in the Bahamas. This time we have no option but to beat there as best we can—unless we choose to bear away through the Windward Passage and go to Jamaica. (I do, in fact, pull out the relevant charts at one point.) It is yet another wet and uncomfortable night for me in the cockpit, with Terrie cradling Pippin down below.

As daylight approaches we make out the lighthouse at Matthew Town, the port of entry (and only town) on Great Inagua. One long tack brings us into a calm open roadstead where at 0930 we anchor in front of the ancient customs house. My log notes: "Very tired. Went ashore and scouted out small harbor. Moved boat around in pm. Problem with chafe with mooring lines—solved by using two lengths of chain where lines crossed dockside (Terrie's idea)."

* * * * *

We find ourselves holed up in Matthew Town for almost a week with the wind never once moving out of the east. It is a dusty little town with few visitors. The island of Great Inagua is substantial—it is the third largest island in the Bahamas—but almost uninhabited, with much of the interior occupied by shallow lakes. It is notable for two things: its salt works, owned by Morton Salt, with 300,000 acres of evaporation ponds, and a flock of over 50,000 flamingoes, the largest in the Caribbean, existing in a symbiotic relationship with the salt works. Both are inaccessible on foot. We attempt to rent motor scooters to tour the island but balk at the $50 a day charge for each one. We track down the wildlife warden, Mr. Jimmie Nixon, to see if he will take us to the flamingoes but he too wants $50.

In a letter to my parents in England, which we find decades later in their papers (sadly, the letters home to Terrie's parents have all been lost), I write: "Dear Mum and Dad, here we are in Great Inagua waiting for a north wind to take us to Haiti or the Dominican Republic. We have hardly seen the Bahamas—every time we dropped anchor the wind would start coming round to the north and we would seize the opportunity to head south as this is hard to do in this part of the world… This town is so sleepy no one even sells postcards—the island is given over to acres and acres of salt ponds where the sea water is let in and allowed to evaporate, and then the salt bulldozed up—one million tons a year!"

Terrie writes to her sister: "We are at the last island of the Bahamas chain. We've covered some 1,400 miles and Pippin and I have been seasick for much of it. We had a rough Gulf of Mexico crossing to Key West with help from Ray and another, thank God, so Pippin and I could just lay there feeling miserable while everyone else did all the work. Then we sailed to Fort Lauderdale and across the Gulf Stream to the Bahamas. The Bahamas have beautiful water, unbelievably blue and crystal clear, but it's too chilly to spend much time in. These islands are scrubby, not even the classic palms you expect to line the beaches. Pippin still talks mounds of gibberish, climbs all over the boat, and waves to all passers-by including birds and the setting sun."

We link up with a visiting American, Johnnie, and sail out to the reef by the lighthouse for a taste of snorkeling in the Bahamas. Over the centuries the reefs of Great Inagua have become the final resting place of several notable treasure-laden Spanish galleons, including the *Santa Rosa* in 1599 and the *Infanta* in 1788. Today's treasure is the marine life: this is our first sight of tropical reef and fish, and we are captivated. As an artist, Terrie is constantly excited by the dazzling array of shapes and myriad colors. Years ago she learned a Japanese technique for printing directly off a fish. On this day Johnnie spears a large parrot fish; over the next couple of days it stays on *Nada* getting softer and smellier as Terrie pulls print after print from it, until finally it is returned to the ocean. It lives today on a number of living room walls.

The following day Lonnie Sutton and crew sail in from Puerto Rico headed north. We join them and split Mr. Nixon's $50 charge so that we can all see the flamingoes. The trip is not a success—we are unable to get close to any birds. However, a little over a year later we are back at the end of nesting season and come upon thousands of these gorgeous birds with their newly hatched offspring. What a sight to see, and such a rare treat. So far as we know there are only four major nesting colonies of flamingoes in the western hemisphere—Great Inagua, Rio Lagartos in the Yucatan, on Cuba, and in southern Spain—and we have been privileged to visit all four.

And now an old wooden schooner, *Mantoya*, with two French Canadians, Gilbert and Luke, breezes in, headed south like us. And like us they too have not planned on coming to Great Inagua, but rather had reckoned on sailing to the Turks and Caicos and from there to Puerto Rico. Between us we don't have a single decent chart of the Dominican Republic—which is now our next obvious port of call! Fortunately, Lonnie has more-or-less what we need (he has no detailed harbor charts) and so we make a trade for a copy of my self-published book on marine refrigeration systems (at least I got rid of one).

We are becoming impatient to leave. The wind eases and Lonnie picks up a forecast of light winds for the next couple of days. We decide to seize this opportunity and make for Puerto Plata, some 200 miles away on the north coast of the Dominican Republic, setting sail at 1500 hours. In just fourteen days we have passed clear through the Bahamas, barely setting foot ashore.

FIRST GENERATION SATELLITE NAVIGATION

In 1987 our satellite navigation (satnav) was based on the transit system that was first deployed by the U.S. military in the 1960s. A number of satellites tracked by the U.S. Navy traveled on well-known orbits, with any orbital changes transmitted to the satellite. This updated information was downloaded to receivers on specific frequencies. Because of the movement of the satellite in relation to the receiver, the received frequency differed slightly from the transmitted frequency in a manner that is defined by the Doppler effect. By tracking this frequency shift over a short period of time the receiver could calculate its position to one or other side of the known position of the satellite. Given several such measurements from different satellites (tracked sequentially), the receiver could calculate its position through a form of triangulation.

There were only a limited number of satellites in the system, resulting in time gaps when none were in view, or when there were not enough to complete the triangulation process. We often went for substantial periods of time without a fix, while the complexity of the calculations resulted in numerous rejected fixes. These calculations also depended on keeping an accurate track of time. It took us months to discover that we had a problem that would cause the internal clock on our receiver to run slow every time our engine was running, giving us increasingly erroneous fixes the longer we ran the engine.

CHAPTER 3
THE DOMINICAN REPUBLIC
FEBRUARY TO MARCH 1987

FROM MATTHEW TOWN ON Great Inagua in the Bahamas we alternately motor and sail close-hauled in predominantly easterly breezes for 24 hours. During the first night, the autopilot breaks once more, reducing us to hand steering. The wind fills in; I change the genoa for the jib and put two reefs in the main. Mid-morning the next day the wind dies; we drop the jib and motor. And then in the afternoon an unexpected moderate cold front passes through, packing showers and gusty northwest winds up to 20 knots. We are now sailing under staysail and mizzen, but *Nada* is hard to balance so I drop the mizzen and put up the jib. Under poled-out jib and staysail I find I can get *Nada* to self-steer at hull speed more-or-less downwind but this results in extreme rolling. Terrie and Pippin are seasick. The wind increases further. I go forward and drop the jib, bundle it up and tie it off to the lifelines so it won't blow or get washed overboard. We continue under staysail alone. As the waves build our motion becomes even more uncomfortable; Terrie and Pippin are once again seasick. Luckily the night closes in and they both doze fitfully, jammed into a berth between the lee cloth and a pile of cushions.

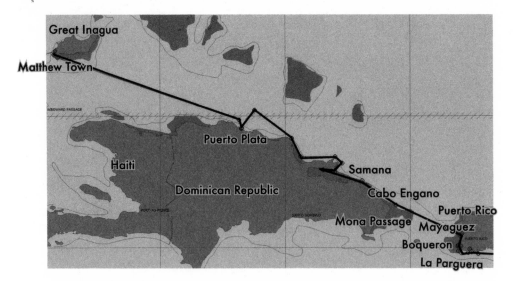

Great Inagua

Matthew Town

WINDWARD PASSAGE

Puerto Plata

Haiti

Dominican Republic

Samana

Cabo Engano

Puerto Rico

Mona Passage

Mayaguez

Boqueron

La Parguera

Sometime during the night the wind eases. We are now a day and a half out of Matthew Town and I have yet to get any sleep. Lethargy creeps over me. The mind registers changes in boatspeed and trim; the body fails to respond. "We're down to four knots; you need to raise the jib again." "I know; I know. I'll get it in a minute." A minute passes and then another. "You really ought to do something about this; you're going to kick yourself if the weather changes and we end up beating just because you failed to make the most of conditions when they were right." "OK, OK. I'll get it in a minute." Another couple of minutes; then a five-minute catnap. "We're down to three and a half knots now; soon we'll be dead in the water. This really is ridiculous." And at some point the mental energy is gathered to kick the body into action. I call Terrie to come and watch the helm.

I move up out of the cockpit to reset the jib. *Nada* is lying fairly quietly so I don't bother to go below to fish a harness and safety line out of the wet locker. I stumble forward without clipping onto the boat, something I have never done before at night. The decks are wet; the boat rolling gently in the leftover swells thrown up by the passage of the front. I start to untie the jib from the lifelines. The boat makes a sudden roll. The next thing I know I am over the side suspended by my armpit from a whisker stay (the stay running from the tip of a bowsprit to the side of a boat), my feet trailing in the water, my head and jaw hurting, with a cut ear, and with no clear idea of how I got there. In the dark night Terrie has no idea I am over the side.

I grab the whisker stay with my free hand and hang there awhile, pulling myself together before working my way back on board. My knees are shaking so badly I can't stand. I sit on the cabintop gingerly feeling my chin and the cut behind my ear. As far as I can tell I was pitched through the lifelines and my head snagged the whisker stay as I went overboard. It was pure chance that my arm was thrown over the stay, giving me a second in which to grab it and almost certainly save my life.

I give myself time to recover somewhat. A few minutes later the jib is set and we pick up boatspeed. The loom of the lights of Puerto Plata comes over the horizon. In another hour or so at 0230 we are hove-to some 5 miles off, awaiting daylight to enter. We have been lucky; for months after Terrie has nightmares in which she wakes up when we are sailing at night to find me gone. She would have been left pregnant and with a baby at sea, with no clear knowledge of where she was, no long-range radio communications (we have only a VHF radio), and no detailed charts.

We did, at one point, consider adding a single-side band (SSB) radio to *Nada* to give us a long-range communications capability. We both studied for the Morse code test that was required to receive a ham radio operating license (this is no longer required), but in the end were deterred by the cost of the radio and its installation and never completed the Morse code test. Later, I grew to like the lack of long-range communications—once we are just a few miles from shore it creates a clear separation between onshore and onboard life—and Terrie has never been bothered about it so to this day we still only have the short-range VHF. Nowadays, when in harbor or at anchor the widespread availability of the internet through wi-fi meets most of our communication needs.

Dawn comes, wet and overcast. The *Sailing Directions* (Volume 144: the Caribbean) for Puerto Plata uses the distinctive mountain behind the town as a range marker, but on this day the mountain is hidden in cloud. The entrance to the harbor lies between two dangerous reefs. We cautiously feel our way in, skirting the reef until we find the channel markers. On the reef to starboard are the rusting remains of a freighter; high and dry on the beach in front of the harbor light is a 92-foot, million dollar yacht minus its keel and with several holes in the hull. We find out this hit the reef to port just a week or so earlier; apparently the skipper tried to enter at night and was being talked in from ashore by someone whom he assumed to be the harbormaster but who was in fact a drunk fisherman—so much for local knowledge.

We are soon safely anchored among a number of other cruising boats and set about tidying up the boat. But then the crew on a neighboring boat tells us that all the boats spin around in different arcs whenever a big barge comes in and out of the harbor so we pull up our anchor to move somewhere with more swinging room. We run aground on a shoal but are able to back off. We move farther out in the harbor and drop our anchor; it drags and has to be retrieved. We finally get a good set with adequate swinging room on its next deployment.

A glance at the satnav before shutting down shows another wildly erroneous fix. And now it finally dawns on me that it is going haywire every time we crank the engine. At first I think perhaps a voltage surge or drop is the problem, but with a little experimenting I discover its internal clock runs fractionally slow when the engine is running. The longer the engine runs, the further behind the clock will get, and the crazier the fixes become. One time it places us in the Indian Ocean! Only months later in Venezuela do I discover that the real culprit is a defective cell in the engine start battery, which is switched into the boat's circuits whenever the engine is running. In the meantime we learn to keep a close watch on the satnav's displayed Greenwich Mean Time (GMT) and to shut the unit down when motoring.

* * * * *

The Dominican Republic shares the island of Hispaniola with Haiti. Puerto Plata is the principal city on the north coast, settled early in the sixteenth century soon after the Spanish conquest but later destroyed on the orders of the Spanish crown because it had become a haven for pirates. Among other things, Puerto Plata is notorious as the site of the British entry into the slave trade when Sir John Hawkins, who had abducted 400 people from Sierra Leone, traded them here in 1563 for pearls, hides, and sugar. Three centuries later, during one of the Dominican Republic's many civil wars, the city was completely destroyed. The current city was rebuilt in the Victorian era.

We have no preconceived ideas about the Dominican Republic. First impressions are not good: we are boarded by half a dozen armed officials and subjected to a great deal of paperwork and rubber-stamping. As we grow more experienced we realize that this excessive paperwork is typical of the ex-Spanish colonies. As far back as the days of the conquistadores and Spanish treasure ships the kings and queens of Spain had an army of clerks recording, and keeping tabs on, every last ducat loaded on and off their galleons. Bureaucratic habits have been deeply ingrained over centuries in all Hispanic cultures.

But despite the guns these are friendly bureaucrats with no trace of hostility and no attempt to extract bribes. And this is something else we are to discover: of all the peoples in the Caribbean, the Hispanics are without question the friendliest, especially where children are concerned. Formalities completed, the officials bum a ride ashore in our dinghy since they have no boat of their own and have been dropped off by another yachtie. We head into town.

The rutted road from the harbor leads through a fence with a 24-hour a day armed guard, across an open sewer, past a foul-smelling rum distillery, and up into the city. Guards armed with shotguns sit on stools outside half the stores. Armed guards are inside the banks and some other stores. We begin to think that Puerto Plata and the Dominican Republic must be in the grip of a wild crime spree or a revolution.

It has indeed had a turbulent history with only rare periods of peace and stability since Columbus first set foot on Hispaniola in 1492. He found an island inhabited by hundreds of thousands of Taino indians. Within a generation slavery, disease, and starvation had all but wiped them out. As early as 1503, just a decade after their invasion, the Spanish were importing

African slaves to make up for the deficit, first to work in the gold mines and later on sugar plantations. The slaves rose up repeatedly, with many fleeing to the mountainous interior and attacking the Spanish in rural areas. French, English and Dutch pirates and privateers raided the cities; in 1586 Sir Francis Drake captured Santo Domingo, the capital, and ransomed it back to the Spanish.

Meantime, the Spanish focus shifted first to Cuba and then to Central and South America; little effort was made to provide strong government. Hispaniola slid into poverty and anarchy. The French seized the western end of the island and established the colony of Saint-Domingue (modern day Haiti), where massive sugar plantations worked by hundreds of thousands of slaves rapidly made it the wealthiest territory in the New World.

The French Revolution precipitated a slave rebellion in Haiti that ultimately resulted in independence. During the Napoleonic Wars in Europe, the Dominican Republic was fought over, and temporarily governed at one time or another, by the French, British, Spanish, Haitians (who sacked several towns, slaughtering most of the inhabitants), and finally the Spanish again. The Haitians re-invaded and initiated a 20-year period of brutal military rule. The Dominicans successfully rose up and achieved independence in 1844, but over the next decade the Haitians launched five invasions; internally the Dominican Republic was plagued by one coup after another.

The Dominicans negotiated with Britain, France, the U.S., and Spain, seeking protection from Haiti. In 1861, while the U.S. was being torn apart with its own civil war and unable to exercise influence in the region, the then Dominican leader negotiated to re-convert the Dominican Republic into a Spanish colony, the first and only time any colony was re-colonized. Within two years a fresh guerilla war of independence broke out. The Spanish abandoned the island, annulling the annexation in 1865, leaving the ruined country in the hands of various regional warlords.

In fifteen years the Dominican Republic suffered through twenty-one governments and over fifty military uprisings. A faction in the U.S. Senate lobbied for annexation, wishing to establish a navy base at Samana on the eastern end of the island. Various corrupt governments borrowed massive amounts from European banks, with the funds then appropriated by the generals and politicians. By the end of the century the national debt was fifteen times the annual budget, with the country on the brink of defaulting. France, Germany, Italy and the Netherlands sent warships to Santo Domingo to ensure repayment of these debts; to head the Europeans off, President Theodore Roosevelt declared that the U.S. would assume responsibility for ensuring that the countries of Latin America met all their obligations.

The U.S. took over control of the Dominican customs in 1905. Following another series of coups with renewed internal strife, the Marines invaded in 1916 and imposed a U.S. military dictatorship. The U.S. sided with the sugar barons in land disputes, dispossessing thousands of peasants, who formed armed guerilla bands. The Marines responded with increasingly brutal counterinsurgency tactics. The U.S. pulled out in 1924.

A brief democratic interlude gave way to the repressive thirty-year dictatorship of Trujillo. He was assassinated in 1961, ushering in another period of instability. In 1965 president Lyndon Johnson, who was at this time getting increasingly embroiled in the Vietnam War and was worried about another Cuba-style revolution in the U.S. backyard, once again sent in the Marines to establish a nominally democratic, but in practice repressive, government that protected American and foreign interests.

By the time we arrive in 1987 there have been several elections with more-or-less peaceful transfers of power, albeit with significant electoral violence and fraud. However, the longstanding tradition of coups, internecine warfare, gangster-ism, and police corruption and repression lies only just below the surface. All those armed guards are not so surprising. Nevertheless, in the weeks we are in the Dominican Republic we never hear of, let alone see, a crime, and never once feel in the least bit threatened, even at night in the poorest quarters of town.

Once clear of the harbor at Puerto Plata we climb past gaily painted wooden houses decorated with intricate woodwork. The street opens out to a handsome square. This is another, charming, Spanish legacy: every town is built around its plaza and in the cool of the evening the citizens turn out, dressed in their best, to wander around and socialize. The plaza is to the Spanish what a pub is to the English. Americans are sadly lacking any equivalent social spaces and institutions.

We take an immediate liking to Puerto Plata and the Dominicans. The town is full of life, friendly people, and pretty houses. Loaded donkey carts trot up and down the streets. A little out of the city center is an open-air market with every conceivable kind of tropical fruit and vegetable. We walk from one end of the city to the other, and everywhere we go Pippin, strapped to one of our backs, attracts friendly curiosity. Time and again we are to find that she is a roving ambassador, collecting friends and offered many a small gift by desperately poor people. Both Terrie and I have a smattering of Spanish; we do our best to express our gratitude and strike up conversations.

Terrie writes to her sister: "Wow, finally after days of seasickness, Paradise! Lush tropical vegetation, mountains rising from the anchorage to 3,000 feet. Brightly colored houses with lots of gingerbread on them like in New Orleans. People Spanish speaking and very friendly and all love children. I've been eating four mangoes daily from the local market…it's wonderful just to be here."

We are taken to a community kitchen in a relatively impoverished neighborhood. We enter a perfectly ordinary looking house and pass through the living room to the back. Here early every morning a group of women begin cooking enormous pots of rice and meat over charcoal fires. Around noon people drift in from all over the area, carrying pots and cans, to collect their lunch. For less than $2 a day we are treated to some of the best food we find anywhere in our travels.

But while we enjoy the town as much as any other we have visited, the anchorage is one of the worst we have stayed in. We spend three weeks in Puerto Plata and on all but a few days an obnoxious swell sets into the harbor, rolling the boats from side to side. At times the swell is so bad that boats tied to the town dock are crashing their spreaders together. At night sparks fly. On at least two occasions various boats suffer thousands of dollars in damage.

And just to cap it all, the harbor is dirty and full of plastic bags, and "every time the wind goes in the east (almost every afternoon) the town power station belches soot all over the boats until the decks have a fine carpet. Just as well I scrubbed them yesterday or the rain in the night would have made a filthy mess."

A huge barge comes into port pushed by two oceangoing tugs. It berths on the cruise ship dock. Twice a week a cruise ship motors in, at which time the tugs take the barge out to sea and bring it back after the liner has left. The tugs come in at right angles to the barge to push it onto the dock, opening their engines wide. The propeller wash sets up a whirlpool in the anchorage, with boats breaking loose left, right and center, bumping into one another and fouling rodes. The first time this happens my log reads: "The wash from the tugs caused a whirlpool in the anchorage—boats all over the place, dragging anchors and fouled propellers, etc. Two boats went over our stern anchor, which then dragged until it hooked someone else's line. Took until noon to sort out." Fortunately no damage is done. We all breathe a sigh of relief when the barge finally leaves.

Some days Pippin wakes in the morning and is seasick before we can get her off *Nada*. For days on end we flee our fine boat at first light, only returning after dark when Pippin is asleep. We hang out all day in the plaza with me babysitting in the mornings while Terrie paints, and Terrie babysitting in the afternoons while I write. In a letter to my parents Terrie reports that she is "getting to paint a little each morning then most afternoons are spent wearing Pippin out in El Parque Central, climbing a tree, playing with other children and helping the shoeshine boys. The market is beautiful. Oh, there are so many places I want to be painting at the same time."

Pippin makes friends with a young street urchin who seems to live in the plaza. Everywhere we go he comes with us. In all the time we are there he wears the same torn and dirty shirt and pants so just before we leave we buy him a new set of clothes. He is so excited he charges out of the store and comes within an inch of being run down by a passing car. When we part, it is with tears in everyone's eyes.

The protracted babysitting and extended walks around town reveal a problem that is to plague us increasingly. Although I had surgery after rupturing the discs in my back in the oilfields, setting back the departure on our cruise by two years, the operation has only been partially successful. Some boat work always gives me problems, particularly cranking in the anchor, making sail changes, and stuffing sails in sail bags. With care, and turning over much of the physical work to Terrie, we are getting by.

But whereas before we set sail we had a stroller to put Pippin in, and a car to drive around in, now Pippin has to be carried everywhere. There is a limit to how much I can load up Terrie—we get the strangest looks when I amble along empty-handed with her following behind with a baby on her back and a heavy shopping bag in each hand! We have yet to see a backpack designed for two babies—once the new baby is born I will have to carry one. In the meantime, my back seems to be slowly deteriorating.

The wind keeps us in port. The Dominican Republic is more or less below the reach of winter northers. We are in the kingdom of the trade winds, blowing relentlessly from the east, and since we need to go east we choose to wait it out. I do various maintenance chores and repair the autopilot once again. We ride up the funicular railway to the mountaintop behind Puerto Plata and enjoy the tropical gardens and panoramic views. We team up with Gilbert and Luke from *Mantoya*, who sail in after us, and rent a car to tour the island—luxuriant, mountainous, and unspoiled but with only a handful of paved roads. I write home describing "large trees of flaming orange blossoms; air plants growing on the telephone wires; lush, rich countryside; small huts thatched with banana leaves; Pippin's first taste of mangoes—she loves them."

Just about anything will grow in the Dominican Republic. We pass huge fields of sugarcane, large cattle ranches, valleys of irrigated rice fields, and mile after mile of coconut groves along the coast. The people are hardworking but desperately poor. We even see a field being ploughed by hand with a wooden plough. We can't help but feel there must be something terribly wrong with a political and social structure that can produce such poverty out of such fertile soil.

We make various trips along the coast by guagua—privately owned mini-buses that provide cheap public transport for much of the island. Guagua rides can be quite an experience. The more passengers, the more the driver makes. It appears they will go anywhere so long as they can fill the bus, and there seem to be no regular bus stops. One man drives while another hangs out the side door hustling business. The horn is blown at every passer-by and detours are made through urban areas until the bus is full. On one ride we have nineteen adults and two children in a twelve-seat bus. The driver is still trying to find more passengers. Pippin is keeping herself amused with a flea-infested puppy and some farmer's pet fighting cock.

In the cities we discover you can flag down passing mopeds for a ride. We only do this once, half in jest. We end up with five people on a Honda motor scooter: Pippin's young friend crouched in front of the driver, the driver, Terrie on the passenger seat behind him, me on the luggage rack with my feet dragging in the road, and Pippin on my back. The driver runs flat out down the center of a busy street, overtaking all the traffic. We walk home.

We are still in town on February 27, the Dominican Republic's Independence Day, a boisterous public festival. The weekend preceding Independence Day gangs of young boys dressed in dazzling costumes and masks come pouring out of the slums carrying inflated cow's stomachs, which resemble large balloons. They collect these from the town's slaughterhouses. The boys race around the plaza beating the girls with these stomachs, making a loud popping noise. There's a great deal of shouting, squealing, and laughing. Each evening the same ritual is repeated in the build-up to carnival day. On the 27th it seems the entire city has turned out for an extraordinarily colorful parade, reminding us of Mardi Gras back in New Orleans.

From the log the next day, Saturday, February 28: "The day got off to a bad start. The wind is firmly back in the east, the boat pitching, and Pippin was seasick... I am getting restless—I have to get to Puerto Rico soon for telephones, mail, and photo development for the deadline on the next book [*Repairs Afloat*, supposed to be ready at the end of March] and being unable to stay on the boat in the daytime is a big strain on all three of us—no one

can work properly and we can't leave Pippin alone for even 30 seconds. In the afternoon we found a children's fancy dress party sponsored by Bermudez—the local rum manufacturer—and took Pippin."

We finally give up waiting on a change in the weather and a couple of nights later, when it seems a little calmer than usual, pull up our anchors—deeply embedded in the mud—and motor out. In 1987 the Dominican government is doing nothing to encourage visiting yachts, restricting sailors to only three ports: Puerto Plata, Santa Barbara de Samana in the northeast, and the capital city of Santo Domingo in the south. There are, in any case, almost no protected anchorages on the north coast. Our objective is Santa Barbara, 120 miles to the east-southeast.

*****

We power out between the reefs only to find the wind dead on the nose, stronger than expected, and kicking up a nasty chop. It is heavy going, with *Nada* periodically hobbyhorsing, crashing up and down and barely moving forward, cutting our already slow speed in half. Terrie becomes seasick. After an hour of this we turn around and motor back in with our tail between our legs. It is nerve-wracking picking our way through the reef in the dark. We are re-anchored at three in the morning.

During the remainder of the night the wind does in fact moderate; we should have pressed on. At daylight two or three other boats make a break for it and we follow them out. Once clear of the harbor we find ourselves beating into a fresh trade wind. We settle down for a protracted windward slog, motorsailing 20 miles offshore and then tacking back into the coast, arriving off Cabo Frances Viejo at dusk. The lighthouse is out of action, which is not uncommon in these waters. We have to make one more tack to round the headland.

The high islands of the Caribbean frequently experience diurnal wind shifts, with onshore winds during the day and offshore breezes at night. During the daytime, the land heats up causing the air to rise, which pulls in wind from offshore, rising to a peak speed in mid-afternoon, often as high as 25 knots. At night, the land cools off, causing air to sink down the face of the mountains and flow out to sea with enough force to cancel out the trade winds along the coastline. This is known as the katabatic effect. The higher the mountains, the stronger the nighttime offshore breezes and the farther their reach. I have read about this.

The Dominican Republic has high mountains along its northern coastline. Using the satnav I hope to creep along the shoreline throughout the night, taking advantage of any wind change. The strategy turns out to be a great success. Before midnight we are coasting along in relatively calm seas (my log notes "the seas subsided to an oily swell"), close reaching at 5 knots, and very pleased with ourselves. But then at 2326 our maverick satnav goes completely on the fritz, locking onto the "last fix" and refusing to budge. No amount of button pushing, cursing, and cautious hammering on it jogs it loose. It remains out of commission until we are able to have it repaired in the Virgin Islands.

Since few areas of the island have electricity there are no lights ashore to guide us. The sky is dark and overcast. I spend an anxious night sailing on dead reckoning, peering into the darkness for any telltale sign of land, fearful that some wayward current will set us into the rocky shoreline.

Somewhere along here in December 1492 Christopher Columbus was also sailing at night on the *Santa Maria* in consort with the *Nina*. The crew was recovering from a marathon party ashore, hosted by the local Taino indians, and presumably not paying much attention. The *Santa Maria* ran irretrievably onto a reef. There were too many men to fit on the *Nina* so a fort was built ashore out of the remains of the *Santa Maria* and thirty-nine men were left behind. When Columbus returned a year later with a fleet of seventeen ships all that was found were mutilated remains and charred timbers.

At 0330 I take in some sail to slow us down. With dawn's first light Cabo Cabron ("Cape Fool"), the northeastern tip of the island, emerges dead ahead, a rugged and majestic sight, the sun's early rays silhouetting its thousand foot cliffs and enormous caves. In the valleys a wispy night mist clings to the tops of the coconut palms as we sail by close inshore, rolling heavily in the confused swells around the headland. Pippin is seasick; my log notes: "Out with the mops and towels; no more time for sightseeing."

Just a couple of hours later we clear Cabo Samana to the south and bear away to enter the Bahia de Samana. What a truly wonderful cruising area we find this to be (and no wonder the U.S. wanted it as a navy base). The mountainsides run straight into the sea, covered with millions of coconut palms. Rocky headlands enclose small bays with white sandy beaches. The few wooden fisherfolks' houses nestling on the beaches blend into the palms. The water is a clear Caribbean blue, the bay sheltered and calm: an unspoiled sailor's paradise (but subsequently, and not surprisingly, home to major tourist resorts).

Santa Barbara de Samana (commonly abbreviated to Samana) lies two or three hours up the bay. Before noon we are anchored; the repaired autopilot has steered flawlessly throughout the trip. In the Dominican Republic it is required to clear in and out of each port (another bureaucratic Hispanic tradition). Where the officials in Puerto Plata were friendly and honest, here it is a different story with the town's military commander trying to extract first a $25 bribe, then a 25 peso bribe (approximately $8), and finally, upon my repeated insistence on a written receipt, giving up with some muttered threats.

During the afternoon the other boats in whose company we had left Puerto Plata straggle in. All had stayed well offshore during the night and experienced 20–25 knot headwinds and steep seas. One had carried away its forestay complete with roller furling genoa and was lucky not to loose its mast; another had to be towed off the rocks around Cabo Samana when the wind died and its engine failed. Last to come in is the old wooden schooner *Mantoya* with our friends Gilbert and Luke aboard. The heavy pounding has opened up several seams and *Mantoya* is taking on water. They had departed Canada armed with a set of private label Imray-Iolaire charts to carry them down the West Indian islands but now sadly conclude that this is as far as they can go. We buy their charts, which are considerably better than our government-issue ones. When they leave it is to go back to Canada.

Samana at this time is a small town with evidence of various failed tourist developments (it has subsequently become a major tourist destination and retirement center). The shopping is nowhere near as good as in Puerto Plata. Some of the people speak English and there is a certain amount of low-key hustling of the yachties, but once clear of the dock the people are as open and friendly as elsewhere in the Dominican Republic. Terrie and Pippin make friends with Chiki, a young mother of two from the barrio near the market. Her husband is a fisherman and they live with various relatives in a tiny dirt-floored shack in a slum neighborhood, but as with everyone else we see are always spotlessly turned out, and in fact frequently put us to shame.

While Terrie and Pippin explore ashore I stay aboard to write. My *Marine Diesel Engines* is beginning to sell well and I am now working on a book that will become *Repairs at Sea*. Everywhere we go I dinghy around anchorages ghoulishly seeking disaster stories, and how they have been resolved. *Marine Diesel Engines* is also beginning to put me on the magazine map. After collecting rejection letters for years (I have enough to wallpaper a small room) I have begun to sell the odd piece.

It is ironic that one of the teachers I most disliked at school is likely substantially responsible for my writing success. When I was growing up there was no such thing as a multiple-choice question—we had to write essays. My history teacher forced us to create and follow a clearly defined structure beginning with an introduction, ending with a conclusion that tied back to the introduction, and with one paragraph and sub paragraph leading logically into the next. For years, I was made to write the equivalent of a 1,500–2,000 word magazine article! And then at university I studied philosophy, which, in its essence, is training in critical thinking. It's for the kid who never stopped asking "Why?" and is the perfect basis for understanding all machinery, which operates entirely on logical principles.

I join Terrie and Pippin on shore. Chiki takes us to see the splendid "saltos" (waterfall) on the Cocos river, a mile or two out of town. A guagua drops us by the side of the road. We follow a small river up through coconut groves a half mile or so to the waterfall. Here the river divides around a rocky outcrop with a gnarled old tree in its center and drops shear into a swimming hole which Terrie and Pippin share with a handful of local children while I take photographs.

The Bahia de Samana is a mating ground for humpback whales and it is the end of mating season. On March 10, Terrie's birthday, a group of us yachties obtain permission from the town commander to go cruising in search of the whales. We take off on a Gulfstar 50 owned by Ferrold and Rita Janvier from Houston, motoring back up the bay. It is to be yet another superb day. Toward the mouth of the bay we come upon two large adults with a baby so young that the adults nudge its head out of the water for it to breathe. We cruise in company with them a boat length away at times. The adults periodically sound and then re-surface with a great "whoosh," sending a column of spray high in the air.

The whales swim alongside and in front of us, seemingly completely unconcerned, and then finally sound for good. We turn for home, but now one of the adults puts on a spectacular display, rolling on its side, waving a huge white flipper in the air, and smacking the water with great force, throwing up a cloud of spray. It is still doing this as we lose sight of it over the horizon. We motor slowly back to Samana, soaking up an early evening view of this marvelous coastline, bathed in an increasingly orange light. A pair of native fishing boats, their sails a patchwork quilt of multicolored cloth, keep us company for a while, and are last seen as a silhouette against the setting sun. It has been a truly red-letter day and a perfect birthday present for Terrie.

We would like to stay longer in Samana, making day trips to explore many of the surrounding bays. In our month-long stay in the Dominican Republic we have made friends both ashore and on other boats. But I have a deadline to meet and need modern mail and phone systems. Late that same evening we pull up our anchor and set sail for Puerto Rico across the notorious Mona Passage.

FOR DAYS CONVERSATION AMONG the boats in Samana has repeat-edly drifted back to the Mona Passage. This relatively shallow, 60-mile-wide body of water between the Dominican Republic and Puerto Rico has a mean reputation. It initiates an uphill slog against the current and northeast trades toward the Virgin Islands. I write to my parents: "The next several hundred miles are likely to be the hardest of all until we reach the Virgin Islands, and then we can start to relax—they call this stretch the 'Thorny Path' as it is mostly beating into the prevailing wind and seas…" With other cruisers we dissect the daily weather forecasts on shortwave radio from the U.S. Coast Guard in Norfolk, Virginia, and the Turks and Caicos radio station. Easterly winds, 15 to 20 knots and maximum swells of 10 feet: not good.

The direct course to the Virgin Islands is almost due east following the northern coast of Puerto Rico with San Juan—the first decently protected anchorage in 210 miles—a hard thrash to windward. Our alternative is to head east-southeast following the rocky Dominican coastline as far as Cabo Engano ("Cape Cheat"), some 70 miles away, skirting a dangerous shallows (a notation on the chart reads "tide rips and heavy swells along the edge of this bank"), and then crossing the Mona Passage to Mayaguez, 140 miles away on the western end of Puerto Rico. In the Mona Passage itself we can expect to find northeast swells generated way out in the Atlantic, piling into the prevailing northwest current to create nasty seas.

From Mayaguez normal practice is to creep along the southern coast of Puerto Rico, exploiting the partial lee provided by the island and sheltering between short hops in the half dozen or so excellent anchorages. We elect to head for Mayaguez and follow the southern route.

We weigh anchors at 2345 and proceed to sea on a clear moonlit night that helps us find our way out of the Bahia de Samana. An hour later we are broad reaching at 5 knots under jib, double-reefed main, and mizzen, a pleasant southerly breeze coming off the land moving us comfortably on our way with little wave action. "0230, running parallel to the coast in 110 to 180 feet of water…Moon clouded over but still enough light to pick out the mountainous silhouette of the land." "0420, moon has set and it is getting very dark." Some anxious moments now. "0430, Fl(2)10sec, 148 degrees magnetic. Should be Punta Nisibon Lt." How kind of this light to work!

During the night and the following day the light wind veers to the southwest and then fills in from, of all places, the northwest: a cold front, so long hoped for, has forced its way this far south. We continue to broad reach and run in near perfect conditions.

A round of morning sextant sights puts us 15 miles north of my dead reckoning—unnerving, as we will be closing Puerto Rico after dark. We press on, debating whether to seize this opportunity to head for San Juan after all rather than Mayaguez. A LAN sight and a round of afternoon sights shot through holes in the increasing cloud cover make no sense. I anxiously rework all the sights and discover that I have been using the wrong assumed latitude. We are dead on track.

As dusk approaches we close Isla Desecheo, glad to have an accurate fix before the final run into Mayaguez and even more glad to have this unlit islet safely behind us before dark. Now a coast guard cutter hails us and comes alongside. This is the age of "zero tolerance." If the coast guard finds as much as the butt end of a marijuana "joint" we can lose our boat. From the beginning of *Nada*'s build process I have been paranoid about this; any time friends have come to visit, if they were smoking a joint I made them throw it away before climbing the ladder to come aboard. In the hot, wet Louisiana environment it was not long before we had marijuana plants growing tall beneath the ladder!

An armed party boards *Nada* and orders everyone up on deck while they search below. I protest and insist on being present during the search. The commanding officer puts his hand on his pistol and orders me out of the cabin. I reluctantly comply. This is our third boarding by the coast guard in the Caribbean and the Gulf of Mexico. There is something wrong with a policy that allows a search of a boat without anyone being present during the search. In spite of the delay, by 2230 we are safely anchored in Mayaguez, *Nada* having made good an average speed of a little over 6 knots in some of the easiest sailing conditions in months. We have been lucky.

Puerto Rico is another of those Caribbean islands discovered by Columbus and settled by the Spanish immediately afterward. Once again, the Taino indian population was more-or-less destroyed within a generation and replaced by imported African slaves. The subsequent history of Puerto Rico is peppered with slave revolts and independence struggles, but is nowhere near as bloody or anarchic as in neighboring Hispaniola. In general, Spain managed to maintain control until its defeat by the U.S. in the Spanish-American War of 1898. Since then, Puerto Rico has been a colony of the U.S. in one form or another. Today the Puerto Ricans are U.S. citizens with a right to elect their own governor but without a vote in either the U.S. Congress or in U.S. presidential elections.

Mayaguez is a necessary port of call for entering or leaving Puerto Rico's west coast, but as an anchorage it is rolly and uncomfortable, the water is filthy, and the air pungent with the smell of fishing boats and fish processing plants. We clear customs the following morning and leave the same day, sailing south a couple of miles off the coast, on a relaxing sunny afternoon.

The wind is astern and the boat on autopilot. I am horsing around with Pippin in the cockpit when I happen to glance at the depthsounder: 8 feet. Astonished, I take a quick look ahead. What is this? A flock of seabirds? Comprehension dawns—the tip of a reef—awash—that is not on our charts. I dive for the tiller, throw off the autopilot, haul in the sheets, and come around in 6 feet of water. It is a narrow escape. Months later in Venezuela we meet a cruising couple that ran up on the self-same reef, becoming wedged for a long nerve-wracking night. Adrenaline is still running high when we slip in between the fringing reef at Boqueron and anchor in the bay.

Boqueron is one of a number of totally protected anchorages we stay in over the next few weeks, some of the best in the Caribbean. Mangroves line both sides of the bay with a sandy, coconut-fringed beach and an inviting town at its head. Inland, mountains draped in tropical vegetation run the length of the island, rising to the lofty 3,500-foot peaks of El Yunque far off in the east.

We dinghy ashore without any great expectations to explore the town. We have viewed Puerto Rico as little more than a stepping-stone on our way to the Virgin Islands and the West Indies. We have subconsciously absorbed the popular American misconception of Puerto Ricans as macho New York hustlers (almost half of all Puerto Ricans live in New York). Instead, we find Puerto Ricans to be some of the friendliest and most compulsively generous people we have met in all our travels. Throughout our month-long stay we are showered with hospitality.

Terrie writes to my parents, "Dear Mum and Pops, we are on the southern coast of Puerto Rico now. Nigel has been anxious to get here for postal and phone service as the deadline nears for his *Repairs At Sea* book. He has been going around different anchorages recording the details of everyone's misfortunes at sea, sounds gory! He's now compiling drawings, photos and text to send off in the next few days…Pippin is still far from being able to swim which we are now trying to spend a little time each day to improve her ability. She is so active it's scary living surrounded by water…"

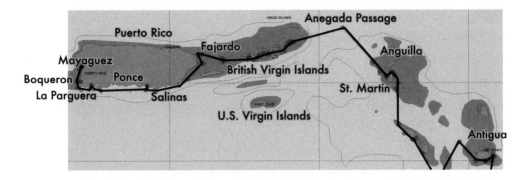

Before leaving Boqueron we take our dinghy and explore small channels in the mangrove swamp to the southeast, seeing numerous herons and snowy egrets. We then motorsail the few miles around Punta Aguila to La Parguera and another lesson in reef navigation. The approach to La Parguera is beset with low-lying islets and a barely submerged reef. The channel twists and turns. As we make our way in we see a sailing boat apparently coming out toward a gap in the islands that I assume to be the channel. I relax my vigilance and make for the "pass" only to find it is all reef and the other boat is anchored on the far side, the crew enjoying some snorkeling.

We work our way around to the same anchorage to join in the snorkeling and put the dinghy over the side. However, *Nada* begins to drag her anchor. After another unsuccessful attempt to get the anchor to bite in the rocky bottom we decide to move into La Parguera and return in the dinghy. We feel our way in through shallow channels with some depths as low as 6 feet, pulling the dinghy behind us (we normally stow it on deck), dropping the anchor almost in the mangroves. Backing down I forget the dinghy is astern and foul the dinghy painter, chewing it up. Here, and later on in Salinas, we have hardly a ripple to disturb us, and only the occasional cruising boat passing through. In our dinghy we are able to wind in and out of the mangroves, through mysterious tunnels formed by the laced-together overhanging branches.

Terrie has developed painfully infected sores in the Dominican Republic, one from a needle prick when making a costume for the Independence Day parade in Puerto Plata. Despite a course of antibiotics, they are refusing to heal.

There is something about the tropics that seems to cause this to happen—you just cannot afford to ignore even little pin pricks and scratches: all must be cleaned, sterilized, and kept clean until healed. We find another doctor and another course of antibiotics but it is to be months before the finger heals and years later it is still uncomfortable. While we are about it, we get Pippin's childhood MMR inoculation.

We have been expecting our friends Lyle and Janet to come and join us but on calling find they are unable to get away. We feel a sense of disappointment with an intensity that surprises us—we have had no mail or communication with family or friends in two months and are missing them more than we realize. Cruising is proving to be quite lonely, and after our rough passages and having to watch Pippin every second of the day we are having mixed feelings about it as a way of life. My back is aggravating the situation—it is giving me a good bit of trouble and I haven't had a decent night's sleep in a month. I am unsure just how much longer we can continue. What will we do if I develop serious problems on one of those long, lonely passages in the Pacific?

I write to my brother and sister-in-law in England: "Dear Chris and Liz, the cruising life so far has been a very mixed affair. Pippin gets seasick, which surprised us—we thought babies were more-or-less immune. Unlike a house where we can set aside a room and make it childproof she needs watching 24 hours a day—there is no relief. She can now climb into every space on the boat. The first day on board I assumed she could not get up the companionway ladder (it is very steep) turned around, and there she was on the top step and fell off at that moment. I actually caught her just before she hit the floor. So then I took the ladder down and next thing she had found various footholds and handholds and was sitting on the chart table playing with all the electrical breakers. When we are heeled under sail on the port tack she climbs in the bookcase and starts pulling books out… and so it goes on. She has also been teething steadily which doesn't help." In my log I note: "Terrie a little depressed—too much babysitting; no art for days (really, since Puerto Plata); no company; bored."

Sailing along the southern coastline to Salinas the next day as the sun comes up, the mountains inland remind us of the foothills of the Rocky Mountains driving through Colorado on Interstate 25 headed for Wyoming. The previous nine years we have spent a portion of every summer in the Beartooth Mountains in Montana backpacking and trout fishing. We wonder whether we will get there this year, and ruminate on how long we want to keep sailing to the next island, what we will do with the rest of our lives, and other such serious thoughts. The log reads: "No conclusions."

The hospitality in Salinas is enough to shake anyone out of an introspective mood, although "Pippin is a little cranky, probably the measles inoculation taking effect." Almost before we are anchored, at his father's insistence a young man comes out in a boat to offer us the run of their house. Domingo and Maria, who run the restaurant at the Marina de Salinas, shower Terrie, who is becoming rather obviously pregnant, and Pippin with gifts. My log marvels at the fact that "Domingo's small rather scruffy-looking garden contains lemons, oranges, papayas, coconuts, sugarcane, pineapples, mangoes, bananas, and two or three other fruits I have never seen or heard of." Another of the patrons at the marina bar drives us to hot springs at Coamo. Domingo and Maria take us to visit her sister in Aibonita where the sister runs a restaurant. She treats us to a fantastic lunch. Afterward they drive us to San Juan to tour the colonial city.

What a magnificent city this is. The old town is well preserved, the Spanish fortifications stretching from one clifftop to another along a coast still redolent of galleons and privateers, cannon smoke, and the crackle of muskets. Here Sir Francis Drake led an unsuccessful assault on his way to a miserable death in 1596. Lord George Cumberland and the Dutch both captured the city of San Juan, but the massive fortress of El Morro never fell until it surrendered to the Americans when they took the island during the Spanish-American War.

We are so taken with Puerto Rico and its people that we make a large dent in our budget to rent a car and tour the interior. We travel the length of the island along the Routa Panoramica that follows the island's mountainous backbone, at one point affording views of both the Caribbean and the Atlantic at the same time. The highpoint of our travels is a visit to the caves on the Rio Camuy, an amazing series of sinkholes and underground caverns only recently discovered and opened to the public. Toward the other end of the island we explore the tropical rainforest in El Yunque National Forest.

In between, I finish the first draft of the book on which I have been working. "Mailed off *Repairs at Sea*! Pippin has just started insisting on feeding herself— a very messy business as the spoon always gets turned upside down before it reaches her mouth. At lunchtime she climbed on the chart table and was feeding her teddy bear (left over egg yolk, naturally!)." A few days later there is another note in my log that reads: "Maria's sister from Aibonita came to visit and brought more gifts (she already gave Terrie maternity dresses). This time she came with a T-shirt for Pippin and a necklace for Terrie. The hospitality is getting a little overwhelming—we shall have to leave!"

We make the run from Salinas to Fajardo (on the east coast of Puerto Rico), our next port of call, at night once again so that Terrie and Pippin can sleep and avoid seasickness and we can benefit from the katabatic effect, especially once we round Punta Tuna at the southeast corner of Puerto Rico, after which we will have to head northeast. This will be directly into the trade winds if we wait until daytime. The coastline is well lit and navigation straightforward until the last 5 or 6 miles when the course runs between a series of reefs in shoal depths of 15 to 25 feet.

Despite my holding down *Nada*'s speed, favorable winds bring us to the last treacherous stretch at 0400 in the dark instead of closer to daybreak as planned. However, I am able to get a line on the powerful Cabo San Juan light. With the hand bearing compass in one hand and the other hand on the tiller, and compensating for leeway, I keep us within 5 degrees of the necessary bearing, safely between the reefs. I have one nasty fright when a large, unlit, mid-channel buoy suddenly looms out of the darkness off our starboard beam and disappears into the night astern—we miss it by a scant 10 feet. The adrenaline keeps me awake the rest of the way into Fajardo. We are anchored by 0600.

It is April 10. We have already dallied a month in Puerto Rico. On April 16 Ray and CC, another friend, are flying into St. Thomas in the U.S. Virgin Islands. They want to be in Antigua for race week, commencing April 25th. And then we hear that my brother and his wife are flying into Antigua from England on the 28th and have booked a flight home out of St. Lucia on May 10. We have some sea miles to cover: it is time to get into high gear once again and head for St. Thomas.

▲ Nigel with Pippin, age eight months, a few months prior to the start of our trip to Venezuela in 1987.

▲ Pippin horsing around in *Nada*'s cockpit. The "dummy" tiller for *Nada*'s autopilot rig is in the foreground.

▲ *Nada*, our 39-foot William-Atkin-designed ketch, at anchor in Puerto Plata.

▲ The Spanish fortifications at San Juan, which we arrived at by car from Salinas.

▼ *Nada* anchored off Soufriere, St. Lucia, tied to a palm tree ashore.

▲ Fishermen hauling in their net off Soufriere, St. Lucia.

▼ A large dug-out canoe being constructed on the riverbank above the Hacha water-falls at Canaima, Venezuela.

▲ The small mountain village of Pinango, Venezuela, finally coming into view.

▲ Naptime for Terrie, Pippin, and Paul – a rare treat aboard *Nada*.

▼ The beach at Pargo, the last village in Venezuela.

▲ Pippin on the beach at Pargo holding a baby monkey.

▲ *Nada* at sea with excessive heeling, side decks awash with saltwater.

▼ Making landfall at Isles des Saintes.

▲ Unspoiled Pinneys Beach, Nevis, now home to a large resort.

▲ A local, inter-island trading boat on its way from Nevis to St. Kitts.

▲ Carnival in St. Kitts.

▲ *Nada* anchored off Culebrita, with Terrie, Paul and Pippin in the foreground.

▲ Haitian fishing boats at Cap Haitian.

▼ The remains of Henri's palace at Sans Souci.

▲ The remains of Henri's Citadelle.

▲ Flamingoes on Great Inagua.

▼ Mountains of salt on Great Inagua.

CHAPTER 5
ANTIGUA OR BUST
APRIL 1987

ALTHOUGH COLUMBUS MADE a water stop in St. Croix, one of the islands in the U.S. Virgin Islands, his landing party was driven off by the native Carib indians. Subsequently, the island escaped sustained colonization until 1555 when the Spanish sent an invasion force which proceeded to annihilate the Caribs. By the end of the century, most were either dead or had fled. The Spanish later ceded St. Croix to the French.

Meanwhile, Dutch and English buccaneers and planters established bases on neighboring Tortola, St. Thomas, and St. John. Tortola was annexed by England, and St. Thomas and St. John by Denmark, which subsequently also purchased St. Croix from the French. Using imported African slave labor, St. Croix in particular developed successful sugar plantations which eventually supported an immensely rich island aristocracy but which went into rapid decline with the freeing of the slaves.

The opening of the Panama Canal gave the Virgin Islands strategic significance in as much as they lie directly on the route from the Atlantic to the canal. In 1917 the U.S. purchased the Danish Virgin Islands (St. Croix, St. Thomas, and St. John) for $25 million. Today, they have a similar status as Puerto Rico, which is to say the inhabitants are U.S. citizens with local self-government but no voice in the U.S. Congress or presidential elections; the British Virgin Islands (Tortola, Virgin Gorda, Jost van Dyke, and Anegada, as well as some smaller islands along the Sir Francis Drake Channel) are a Crown Colony, with a governor appointed by the British Government, and advised by an elected council.

More-or-less midway between Puerto Rico and the Virgin Islands lies Culebra. A gentle motorsail brings us to its western coast and an anchorage off the little town of Dewey. The next day a wind shift to the south sets us rolling at anchor; we move around to the totally protected bay of Ensenada Honda where we encounter a number of other cruisers.

Pippin never sleeps through the night and is crying a fair bit. In one way or another, we still spend a good deal of time holding her. We are new parents and not sure how to handle this. In fact, we had not been sure whether or not we wanted children in the first place but Terrie's biological clock was running out so we decided she would stop taking the pill and we would see what happened. She had forgotten the pill numerous times before so we didn't expect much but instead she instantly became pregnant and now we have Pippin. We decided one child would be lonely, hence Terrie's current pregnancy.

I see an older sailor, well into his sixties, pottering around the anchorage in a dinghy with two young children. I ask him how he deals with the children when they are crying. Peter invites me over to his boat to find out. It is a 50-foot, home-built, engineless wooden yawl. He shows me something close to a jail cell built into the bow of the boat. "I just put them in there and let them cry themselves to sleep." Behind him is his teenage wife, Florence, with their 4-month old daughter whom he insisted on delivering himself on the boat because the local hospital refused to allow him to be present at a hospital birth.

Peter enthusiastically says he would like to have six children. Florence is looking pale and washed up, and shaking her head "No." Only later do I realize that this is the famous Peter Tangvald who later lost his life and that of one of his children when he ran his boat onto a reef off of Bonaire in the middle of the night. Fortunately, Florence, his sixth wife (two of whom were lost at sea) had left him by then, taking her daughter, Virginia, with her. We continue to hold Pippin when she cries.

A day or so later and another gentle motorsail sees us entering Charlotte Amalie, the capital of St. Thomas in the U.S. Virgin Islands. The excitement is palpable. We have always viewed these islands as our first major objective. We have all but completed the windward leg of our voyage, having made good 1,500 miles to the east against the prevailing winds and currents. A couple more passages to Antigua, no worse than a dozen we have already made, and we will be "turning the corner" in the Caribbean, reaching and running first south to Venezuela and then westward to Panama and across the Pacific. Crew morale has never been higher. We are in for a rude shock.

The first shock is Charlotte Amalie itself. What a hustle and bustle with hundreds of yachts and up to eleven cruise ships disgorging thousands of passengers a day. After our leisurely two months in the Dominican Republic and Puerto Rico this is hard to take. There are no beaches and the harbor is too polluted for swimming. Prices of basic supplies are high and service is poor. Terrie paints the fish market in French Town. She writes to my parents of "the ladies in their straw hats waiting for the boats. Boy, don't get in their way when the fish get plunked down—it's tooth and nail." We stay long enough to have the satnav repaired and to pick up Ray and CC from the airport, and then beat a hasty retreat, first to St. John and then to Virgin Gorda.

Ray and CC bring diving gear and want to get in at least one dive in the Virgins so we take them to Round Rock off the southern end of Virgin Gorda. It is not a success. The day is windy and there are heavy cross swells. CC is pushing me to go unsafely close to the rocks. We punch a hole in the side of the dinghy and nearly swamp it when a wave throws it up against *Nada*. Once the two of them are in the water we pull away and roll around for forty minutes until they come back up. The dive itself is nondescript. But at least it teaches me one thing—a sailboat does not make a good dive platform; people who want to go diving should go out with the pros.

We need to be on our way to Antigua (in the Lesser Antilles), 180 miles to the southeast. It is mid-April. Already the trade winds are shifting from their more northerly winter track toward their summer path south of east, putting us on a dead beat to windward. To make matters worse, the Caribbean arm of the North Equatorial Current—the Antilles Current—flows up in a generally northwesterly direction past Antigua and St. Martin, and then westerly around the Virgins both to the north and south. It, too, is dead against us. Unfortunately, having locked ourselves into other people's schedules we are not in a position to wait for a favorable weather window.

Donald Street in his seminal *Cruising Guide to the Eastern Caribbean* recommends making as much progress eastward as possible in the lee of Virgin Gorda before striking out across the Anegada Passage. We reach up the back of Virgin Gorda in sheltered water, round Necker Island to the north, and tack out into the Anegada Passage; that's where the work begins.

The wind is on the nose at 10 to 15 knots—not particularly strong but just enough to kick up a nasty short chop which, together with the prevailing swells, periodically sets *Nada* to hobbyhorsing, reducing our speed to less than 3 knots. With the current running against us, attempts to loosen the sheets, bear away a few degrees, and pick up boatspeed have us tacking through such a wide arc that we are no better off. In any case, the motion is not much improved due to the confused seas.

Pippin is seasick; Terrie is looking green. At our current rate of progress, we are faced with a grueling two-day slog just to get to St. Martin with Antigua as far again in the same direction. Ray and CC, with limited vacation time and heads filled with visions of party time at Race Week, are far from happy. Crew morale is sinking as fast as it had risen a few days previously.

We crank the iron genny, pinch up the boat, and motorsail doggedly into the night, slogging away at a steady 4½ knots at just a little above idling RPMs. This is a wearying way to travel, adding the heat and noise of the engine to an already uncomfortable motion. Every once in a while a stronger gust hits us and rolls *Nada*'s rail under; the engine oil pump suction line pulls in air and the oil pressure momentarily drops off, resulting in an alarming clatter from the engine. Between worrying about the engine and concern that the crew will steer off course, which is easy to do when close-hauled, I find myself unable to sleep.

We stay well north in the Anegada Passage, making toward Sombrero Island, as Street reckons this avoids the worst of the current. But even with the motor, adding in leeway and the current, we are making no better than 120-degree tacks over the bottom. Toward dawn we pick out the powerful light on Sombrero and come about toward Dog Island. Set to the west once again, we make another tack up behind Dog Island and finally escape the worst of the current.

Things improve. In the partial lee of Anguilla the seas are more uniform and *Nada*'s speed increases by a full knot. A tack between Anguilla and St. Martin puts us in position for one last beat into the Baie du Marigot, on St. Martin. We drop anchor as the last glow of evening light fades in the west; it has taken us 30 unpleasant hours to cover a rhumb line of less than 80 miles.

In the morning we find St. Martin to be "very French; good brie and pâté. Ooooh the pastries…" but we have no time to enjoy it. None of us are looking forward to the 100-plus mile slog to Antigua. The wind is still south of east. We plan to head for St. Christopher (St. Kitts), creeping down the lee side of that island and Nevis; this will put us as close to Antigua as possible for the final uphill beat. To further improve our angle relative to the wind I decide to leave St. Martin at dusk, making our way around the northern and eastern coasts into the lee of St. Barthelemy, and only then crossing to St. Kitts. With any luck we will encounter lighter winds and calmer seas at night, Pippin will sleep through the trip and not get seasick, and we will be at Basseterre, the port of entry for St. Kitts, soon after daybreak.

We leave Baie du Marigot at 1800 hours, almost exactly 24 hours after arriving. As we pass Rocher Creole toward the northwest tip of St. Martin night settles in, dark and overcast with no moon, making our distance off the coast hard to judge. Ahead of us are the dangerous unlit Spanish Rocks, roughly three-quarters of a mile offshore. We work our way around the coast, staying just within the 10 fathom line because the water between the coast and the rocks is charted at 10 fathoms; so long as we keep below this depth I have no fear of straying too far offshore and running afoul of the Spanish Rocks.

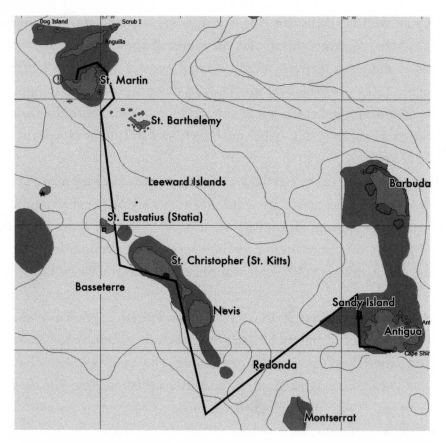

Once clear of the rocks we continue close-hauled toward St. Barthelemy. We pass between St. Martin and the island of Tintamarre, one mile offshore, but the night is so dark we never even sight the island. The southeast coast of St. Martin is bedeviled with a series of unlit rocks and small islands. We hold hard on the wind to clear them by a couple of miles.

Ahead on this course lies another series of unlit islands off the coast of St. Barthelemy. What I don't know is how much current, if any, we are contending with, and what its set is. We have enough open water on our intended track to allow for up to 1½ knots of current setting us anywhere from the west to the north (the most likely directions) but no more. The satnav chooses this night to reject all fixes for seven hours—I swear the beast knows when I can use it most and turns itself off.

The lights of St. Barthelemy vaguely illuminate the horizon. Momentarily I see an island silhouetted off our port bow. I bear away sharply and run off downwind toward open water. In the conditions it is impossible to tell how close we are, but I suspect that we have received a slight southerly lift that has set us uncomfortably close to the island of Roche Table. With the Groupers still to clear I am not in the mood for taking chances and continue downwind until we are safely over the 20-fathom line. In doing so I trade away most of the benefit we have gained from working to the east of St. Martin.

We have another night on the wind with the Antilles Current setting us to the northwest. At 0130 we pick out the lights of St. Eustatius (Statia) off the starboard bow. With a brief push from the motor we are able to squeak around the southeast corner of the island, a scant quarter of a mile offshore, without having to tack. At first light we sail into the lee of St. Kitts. As the sun rises we motor close inshore to Basseterre, our spirits buoyed by the eye-catching tableau ashore of vivid green sugarcane fields framed by impressive mountains.

This is the opening day of Race Week at English Harbour on Antigua—we are late. We spend the day exploring ashore and then at dusk set sail once again for what we all hope and expect will be the last hard beat for months to come. We take advantage of the lee of St. Kitts and Nevis, but all too soon emerge from the shelter of the islands. The wind and seas kick up, the sheets are winched in, and the familiar slog begins again. The wind is solidly in the east; we sail southeast toward Montserrat.

The Antilles Current is running in a westerly direction between Nevis and Montserrat. From being just off *Nada*'s port bow we watch the loom of the lights of Montserrat depressingly ease on around to the port beam. The satnav confirms that we are making over 20 degrees of leeway. At 0100 we go onto the starboard tack and make for the northeast.

Between Nevis and Montserrat lies Redonda, a sheer-sided, 1,000-foot, unlit, uninhabited slab of rock rising straight out of the ocean. I feel I have made adequate allowance for leeway, aiming to pass 2 to 3 miles to the east. Using the loom of the lights from Montserrat to get a rough line of position (LOP) with a hand bearing compass, I know we are moving into the danger zone.

I have taken this watch because of the proximity of Redonda, assuming the satnav would provide me with adequate fixes but it is stubbornly blank. I am telling myself, "You need to tack back to the southeast to give yourself a little more room." But after two somewhat sleepless nights I am gripped by lethargy once again and keep delaying, reluctant to make the effort to bring *Nada* around, and assuming I will get that all-important fix. And then I leave it so late that I am worried we may already have been pushed to the west of the island in which case I may tack straight onto it. Where is that fix?

I sit in the cockpit, the autopilot working the tiller, fighting off sleep. My head drops to my chest and snaps back up. And there for a brief instant off the port bow is the mass of Redonda, just a shade blacker than this black night. I jump up and screw up my eyes to drive away the tiredness and focus better. Is this just my overheated imagination hallucinating with lack of sleep? But no, there it is again, just the dimmest outline. I watch it move past and a few minutes later it merges into the night for good.

Five minutes later the satnav comes up with a fix. We have passed Redonda a half-mile off—much too close for comfort in the circumstances. The damned Antilles Current. The current continues to set *Nada* well to the west of Antigua. Soon after dawn we come up on soundings with still no sight of land. Another tack back to the southeast. And then at 0945 Antigua emerges from the haze dead ahead. Ah, Antigua—we have never been so pleased to make a landfall. We breeze down the west coast in calm, protected waters, but we are not quite through.

English Harbour, our destination and the headquarters for Race Week, is on the southeast coast of the island. We have one last beat to make along the southern coast directly to windward. Impatient to get there we crank the motor and try powering straight into the seas. *Nada* takes to violently hobbyhorsing and our speed falls to 3 knots. Reluctantly we bear away and motorsail the remaining miles.

We round Snapper Point, the final headland before English Harbour, dropping the sails as we come past the Pillars of Hercules. I am in the cockpit reading Street's account of the difficulties of entering English Harbour under sail. At this precise moment the engine dies; all the motorsailing from the Virgins has finally emptied our small 30-gallon tank of diesel.

Rushing to reset the jib we pick up a short-lived breeze. This pulls us off the cliffs after Snapper Point and then dies. I am anxiously looking for enough clear space in the outer harbor for us to drop our anchor, but the area is jammed full of boats for Race Week. Another puff pushes us around the reef off Charlotte Point at the mouth of the harbor. Dead ahead is a large three-masted schooner; to starboard a little open water. We drift into the open water and drop our anchor and sails together, a little too close to the schooner for comfort.

But now comes a slightly more sustained puff. I decide to try and raise the anchor and move into a better location. Up with the sails again but the anchor fails to break loose before the gust dies. General confusion ensues—I should have left well enough alone. We drop the sails for the third time, put the dinghy over, row out an anchor on a long rode, and kedge ourselves clear of the schooner.

We have arrived.

* * * * *

Ray and CC take off into town to party. They meet up with a female doctor and the three of them proceed to do some serious drinking, with Ray and CC competing for the doctor's attention and CC getting the better of it. She begins talking about her love life: she has two boyfriends, one of them a New York bisexual and the other a Haitian, and she is in mortal fear of catching AIDS. Before Ray and CC can make an exit, she has one drink too many and vomits all over CC's feet. That finishes the evening; we hear them stumbling back aboard in the early hours. At breakfast the next day Ray is gleefully recounting the story. Just as he reaches the punchline Pippin, who is wandering around without a diaper, squats down and craps neatly on the top of his foot!

Although Columbus visited Antigua, it escaped the Spanish colonization efforts. The island was not permanently settled by Europeans until British sugar barons introduced plantations and slavery in 1632, forcing the native Carib indians into bondage. The indians died by the thousands until they were annihilated. African slaves were imported to replace them. Various nascent slave revolts were savagely repressed, the leaders executed with medieval barbarity.

The sugar plantation owners built up a profitable illegal trade with the American colonies and then, following the American War of Independence, with the nascent U.S. This trade was obstructed by, among others, Horatio Nelson, the Senior Naval Officer of the Leeward Islands from 1784 to 1787. It was further disrupted during the Napoleonic Wars. With the abolition of slavery the sugar plantations went into decline. In the ensuing decades the island experienced a certain amount of civil unrest, but nothing to equal that of some of the Spanish colonies. It gained its independence in 1968.

During the Napoleonic Wars Nelson rose to the rank of admiral. He chased a French fleet from Europe to the West Indies and back, finally cornering it, and the Spanish fleet, at the Battle of Trafalgar, where he was killed. The British either destroyed or captured the combined French and Spanish fleets, establishing British worldwide naval supremacy for the next century. The dockyards on Antigua, built in the 1700s and designed to provide a base for the British West Indies fleet, were re-named in honor of Nelson. Many of the seventeenth century buildings in Nelson's Dockyard have been lovingly restored.

The Race Week fleet takes off for the night, easing the congestion somewhat so that we are able to make our way onto the dock, tank up with diesel and water, and explore ashore. And then it is time to meet my brother, Chris, and his wife Liz, at the airport.

We drink cocktails on the quayside, allowing Pippin to eat the cherries, forgetting that they are soaked in alcohol. She becomes quite drunk. It is only when she begins staggering around that we realize what is happening. We take her back to *Nada*. With the arrival of Chris and Liz we are getting crowded. We have designed *Nada*'s cockpit such that the table can be used to close off the footwell, leveling the cockpit area into enough space for two people to sleep in relative comfort on the cockpit cushions. Chris and Liz camp out here—he in his very British pajamas and she in her nightie.

We sail to Nonsuch Bay on the east coast, finding a delightful anchorage behind the reefs in the lee of Green Island. Ray and CC come up with conch and a huge stone crab; Terrie prepares stuffed peppers. We pop the corks on a couple of bottles of excellent French wine and eat a gourmet meal under the cockpit awning in idyllic surroundings as the sun sets in a blaze of glory.

Antigua is reputed to have 365 beaches—one for every day of the year. A month could be spent working around the island. However, perusing the charts of the West Indies we realize that Chris and Liz's scheduled departure from St. Lucia in eleven days leaves us a lot of ocean to cover in a short space of time. Antigua will have to wait. We deposit Ray and CC in English Harbour, clear out with customs, and set sail for Guadeloupe.

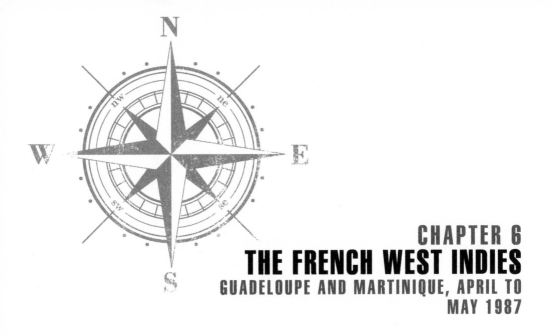

CHAPTER 6
THE FRENCH WEST INDIES
GUADELOUPE AND MARTINIQUE, APRIL TO MAY 1987

AT LAST WE HAVE a perfect trade wind reach as we head south from Antigua with blue skies above, ultramarine waters below, and spray glistening in the air as the ever-present northeast swells roll by. Flying fish break out of wave faces, gliding in formation on gossamer wings along the troughs. This is how I had always thought it would be. Soon after Antigua melts into the haze astern the tips of the mountains of Guadeloupe come over the horizon ahead. From now until we leave Grenada for Venezuela we are almost never out of sight of land.

Although Columbus visited Guadeloupe and Martinique in 1493, as with Antigua, both escaped sustained European colonization until a French invasion in 1635. In just a few years this resulted in the slaughter of the native Carib indians on Guadeloupe; it took a quarter century of brutal conflict to exterminate, or drive off, the Caribs on Martinique. African slave labor was used to develop lucrative tobacco, coffee, and sugar plantations; the white plantation owners became extremely wealthy.

During the Seven Years War from 1759 to 1763 the English captured Guadeloupe and Martinique. At the war's conclusion, France regained control of the islands in return for ceding French Canadian territories to the British.

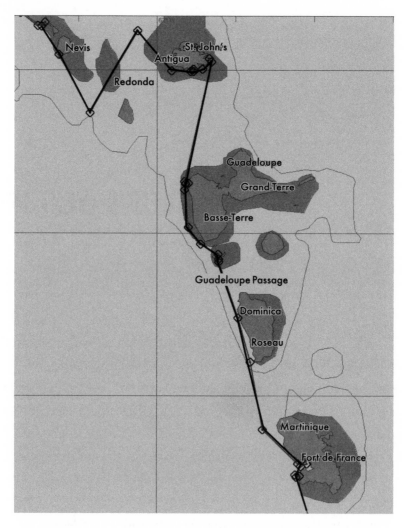

This was in spite of the fact that Canada was considered to be more-or-less worthless by many in contrast to the French sugar islands that were extremely wealthy. The settlement was driven through the British Parliament by the sugar magnates on the British islands of St. Kitts and Nevis in order to remove competition within the British Empire from Guadeloupe and Martinique. The power of special interests was as strong then as it is today!

The French Revolution in 1789 ushered in a tumultuous period of invasions, changes of imperial control (between France, England and even Sweden), slave rebellions, guillotining of the aristocracy on Guadeloupe, freedom for the slaves, and re-enslavement. Hurricanes, earthquakes, and volcanic eruptions have wrought additional periodic havoc. The combined impacts on the sugar plantations of the final ending of slavery in 1848 and the vagaries of the international sugar market resulted in prolonged periods of hardship. Today, sugar production is augmented with bananas and tourism.

Guadeloupe consists of two islands more or less joined together—Grand-Terre to the east (Big Land), which is low and flat, and Basse-Terre (Low Land), which is high and mountainous! We head for Deshaies, a port of entry on the northwest coast of Basse-Terre. A rain shower blots out the mountains as we close the island, and then clears to leave a spectacular rainbow lighting up the jungle in vibrant color. Is this really our pot of gold at the end of the upwind struggle from New Orleans?

We round high cliffs and the bay of Deshaies opens before us, at its head a small fishing town with wooden houses set almost on the beach amongst coconut palms and sea grapes (a species of broad-leaved flowering plant found on many Caribbean beaches), the fishing boats drawn up in front of the houses, nets hung out to dry. We anchor and dinghy ashore to eat a meal, more Creole than anything we have ever found in New Orleans, served up in a little restaurant set over the water. As the sun slips into the sea it sets the town and mountains behind afire with red and orange.

The following morning we clear customs and what an ordeal this turns out to be. The customs office is a stiff walk up a hill and out of town to the south. There are two officers, one friendly, the other hostile, both speaking only French. The hostile one notes that we have an American boat that has only a Louisiana state registration and no coast guard documentation. He wants to fine us 700 Francs (well over $100). I explain in very bad, poorly remembered, schoolboy French that although the boat is American, as a British citizen I am not permitted to have coast guard documentation and that therefore it is impossible for the boat to have it. The friendly officer intercedes on our behalf but the hostile one is quite adamant and produces a copy of his regulations. Sure enough, there it is: all U.S.-registered boats over 5 tons (we are closer to 18) must be coast guard documented or pay a 700 Franc fine.

I run back to the boat and return, sweating and out of breath, with the coast guard Report of Boarding handed to us after our inspection off the coast of Puerto Rico, and our FCC radio license, issued by the federal government. Both have impressive government stamps. The two officers can read neither but nevertheless after some further argument between them *Nada* is admitted. We are told that if we ever come back without coast guard documentation it will mean an immediate fine.

Now it is our turn. We produce our passports. Terrie and Pippin are traveling on American passports. "Where are the entry visas?" Ever since the days of General de Gaulle the French have been somewhat hostile to Americans and periodically require Americans to obtain visas prior to visits to French territory. We are in one of these periods. Chris, Liz, and myself, traveling on U.K. passports, are OK—as members of the EEC (European Economic Community, the forerunner of the European Union) we have free run of any French territory. Some more regulations are produced and a threat made to deny us entry. But then the friendly officer intercedes once again: since I am the "head of the household" and Terrie and Pippin are my "dependents" they should not need visas. This chauvinist charade (I am glaring at Terrie to keep her quiet) finally does the trick and we get our clearance papers—it has taken four hours.

We take the bus to Pointe-a-Pitre, the capital city situated on Grand-Terre. The city itself is dreary and uninteresting, but the ride through fields of sugarcane backed by mountains draped in tropical rainforest is gorgeous. Terrie attempts to paint the scene at the open market but is abusively driven off—something she has never encountered either before or since. We are to find that where the Hispanic islands are the friendliest, in so far as generalizations and first impressions are valid, the French are the least friendly (which is not to say that we don't meet friendly people, because of course we do).

From Deshaies we motorsail south, close inshore, toward the Iles des Saintes. We find Guadeloupe, in common with most of the high islands in the Caribbean, has an enchanting coastline of mountains and luxuriant green jungle. The winds are light and variable: non-existent off the mountains but funneling down the valleys, coming at us from every direction. The short crossing from Basse-Terre to the Iles des Saintes is a beat to windward, open to the ever-present northeast swells driving in from the Atlantic.

The Iles des Saintes are a picturesque group of islands with several good anchorages, pretty beaches, and a neat little town at Bourg des Saintes. In these idyllic surroundings was fought one of the decisive naval battles of modern times. It was 1782. De Grasse, the French admiral who had, the year before, blockaded the Chesapeake and made possible the American victory over Cornwallis at Yorktown, was rampaging through the British-owned islands in the West Indies, capturing one after the other. The great British admiral, Rodney, finally caught up with him. After three days of fighting and maneuvering both de Grasse and his flagship were captured and the French fleet defeated. With one massive blow Rodney reversed a string of British defeats suffered in the Caribbean during the American War of Independence and secured British dominance over the islands for many years to come. What an awesome sight it must have been to see those great, ponderous wooden battleships maneuvering off these islands amidst the smoke and cannon fire.

We anchor off Ilet a Cabrit, making a little smoke of our own, barbecuing over an open fire on the beach. We are joined by a dozen hungry feral cats hovering on the edge of the pool of light cast by our kerosene lantern and fighting over scraps and bones. Pippin is in heaven.

Another day sees us in another beautiful anchorage in the lee of a headland called Pain de Sucre: a classic coconut-fringed sandy beach with nets spread out on a small jetty to dry, complete with topless bathing beauties, the latter quite a surprise since most Caribbean islands are conservative. But then this, of course, is French. We enjoy a lazy day on the beach with Liz giving Pippin swimming lessons.

* * * * *

Dominica is next in the Leeward Islands, after which comes Martinique. As the various imperial powers fought over these islands they changed hands repeatedly. In the final settlement Guadeloupe and Martinique both went to France but Dominica stayed with the British. The practice of the ruling countries was to establish strong tariff barriers to discourage trade with any but the mother country: an island like Dominica would have had far stronger commercial relations with England than with either of its neighbors just 20 miles away. Even with independent governments in most of the islands this sense of isolation is still prevalent. Each has its own customs and entry procedures and checking in and out is one of the necessary frustrations of moving from island to island. After all the problems we have had in entering French-owned Guadeloupe, and given our limited time, we decide to give Dominica a miss and instead proceed directly to Martinique, another French-owned island, setting sail in mid-afternoon.

The short crossing to Dominica in strong winds and confused seas is boisterous. Before we make the lee of Dominica both Terrie and I are seasick. At nightfall we enter sheltered water, keeping close inshore with the moon, stars, and lights ashore giving us a reasonable view of the coastline. However, we have a price to pay for our comfort: the wind varies from east to southwest and from flat calm to 20 knots. One moment we are motoring; the next making 7 knots under jib and mizzen alone. The sails go up and down, the motor on and off, the boat from port to starboard tack. No one gets much sleep.

The southern end of Dominica is sparsely inhabited and the lights onshore few and far between. The island curves a little eastward and then hooks to the west, culminating in the somewhat notorious Scotts Head. The cloud cover steadily increases, the moon sets, we are beset by a series of heavy squalls, and the night becomes black. Unsure of the accuracy of our charts, we give up a considerable amount of our precious easting to head well offshore and be certain of giving the rocks off the headland a wide berth.

As we move out of the lee of Dominica the wind and seas build and we are hard on the wind in an uncomfortable chop superimposed on the underlying open ocean swell. We beat through the rest of the night to Martinique and are still set almost 12 miles to the west by leeway and the Antilles Current. Chris and I sit in the cockpit alternately dozing and chatting while the others try to sleep below. Suddenly Chris leaps up in alarm and cries out: "What the hell was that; something hit me in the back of the head." An unusual noise is coming from the cockpit. We grab a flashlight and investigate: the largest flying fish that has come aboard to date is thrashing and flopping about on the cockpit grate. Terrie has been woken by the commotion; before we can pitch the fish overboard she yells, "Don't put it back; put it in the fridge. I'll print it tomorrow!"

One long tack brings us into the shelter of Martinique, sailing past St. Pierre, the former capital, which was totally destroyed by the eruption of Mount Pelee in 1902. Twenty nine thousand people died; only two survived, one of whom was a prisoner in a dungeon with a single small window. We make our way down to Fort-de-France. This is a truly French city. Whereas other colonial nations have slowly ceded independence to their colonies, the French have integrated theirs into the imperial nation. The citizens of Guadeloupe and Martinique are French citizens, with as equal a vote in French affairs as any other citizen, and with their own representatives in the French National Assembly. Fort-de-France has an air of Paris about it, with plenty of fine Parisian stores, and everyone, black and white, elegantly dressed and very Gallic in appearance.

In the city center is a park dotted with stately royal palms and numerous tropical plants. Nearby is, in Terrie's opinion, "a pastry shop as close to heaven as I'll ever get." After a breakfast of coffee and the finest croissants we have at any time eaten the others go shopping while Pippin and I head for the park. I lie on the grass with Pippin asleep on my chest, gazing through the delicate tracery of the leaves on a gnarled old tamarind tree, watching humming birds at work, fanned by a balmy trade wind breeze, and thinking serious thoughts.

In spite of shuffling most of the hard boat work off onto first Ray and CC, and then Chris, for the past three weeks my back has been acting up. There is also the recent bout of seasickness between the Iles des Saintes and Dominica. The perfection of the surroundings add poignancy to a conclusion taking shape in my mind that I have for some time been trying to avoid: there is no way I can take Terrie and Pippin and a soon-to-be new baby into the Pacific with its long passages in that vast empty ocean.

I continue to wrestle with this issue and its ramifications for weeks as we work our way ever farther south. Giving up on the South Pacific is a deathblow to dreams cherished since my early teens and which provided the principal goal and driving force motivating the eight years spent building and preparing *Nada*, specifically constructed and equipped with a Pacific circumnavigation in mind.

In the meantime, there is today to live for, and Martinique is another intriguing island. We explore the immediate environs of Fort-de-France. On a subsequent visit the following year, after Paul is born, we are able to take taxi collectif (TC) trips around the island (taxi collectif—the French equivalent of a guagua but much more subdued and civilized). Our favorite trip is to Grand Riviere, the most northerly settlement. The scenery the last few miles is impressive, the road twisting through hillsides clad in tropical forest and bamboo, before winding down to Grand Riviere, a little fishing town at the foot of dramatic cliffs with stone houses anchored to rocky outcrops on the beach. The prevailing swells sweep in from the Atlantic, thundering up the pebbly beach and bursting in clouds of spray around the rocks on which the houses are built. The local fishing boats are drawn up just above the surf line on a tiny handkerchief of beach. The heavy boats are launched and retrieved by hand through the surf—a dangerous undertaking requiring courage and skill. We watch a couple of boats come in through the surf to land, each with a meager haul of flying fish after a long night's fishing.

On this second visit, we spend all but our return taxi fare on a delicious meal and then miss the last taxi back to Fort-de-France. We appear to be stuck for the night with two small children (Paul is just five months old) and hardly a penny in our pockets. We sit disconsolately by the roadside trying to hitch a ride when our original taxi driver comes by with his family and gives us a lift to the nearest town. From there we are able to hitch another ride down the coast, finally linking up with a taxi back to Fort-de-France.

Our driver is a strange fellow indeed. He has an obsession about shutting his car doors softly. Whenever a passenger enters and pulls a door to, he jumps out, carrying on in French, reopens the door, and closes it with a gentle push. We pick up a woman by the roadside and go through the same routine. However, he fails to fully latch the door and while he is driving down the road the woman reopens it and closes it with a good hard pull. He slams on his brakes, jumps out, rushes around, re-opens it, and closes it once again, a torrent of obviously abusive French pouring out; he continues to insult the woman as he drives on. I am trying to figure out a way to intervene when fortunately a Frenchman steps into the fray. At this point things really warm up until our driver stops abruptly in the middle of nowhere and orders the man out. In spite of this the man offers to pay for his ride and the driver refuses payment. This offends the passenger's Gallic pride and so they then have a row about this until the driver jumps in and takes off, driving like a maniac all the way to Fort-de-France. We are relieved to arrive in one piece.

However, this is on another occasion. For now, with Chris and Liz we clear customs (very friendly and relaxed here) and sail the short distance across the bay from Fort-de-France and around the corner to Grand Anse d'Arlet with a delightful fishing village framing a lovely palm fringed beach. Lined up on the sand are dugout canoes used by the local fishermen. We are to see them from now on all the way to Grenada.

To make a canoe a large tree is felled and hollowed out, leaving a solid piece thrusting forward some 15 inches at the bow on what would be the waterline. This is fitted with an iron shoe and owes its origin, I believe, to rams on the prows of Carib Indian war canoes, from which these dugouts are derived. The hollow log is set on trestles and filled with rocks and water. A fire is lit beneath it. The heat, water, and weight of the rocks cause the log to sag in the middle, spreading its sides and producing handsome, rockered lines. The log is then fitted with ribs to hold its shape and an extra strake (plank) is added to each side to double its freeboard. The resulting canoe is strong, seaworthy, and able to carry a considerable load. In the early days of the European invasion and colonization of the West Indies canoes were seen that could carry 100 warriors who could paddle faster than ships could sail. The Caribs were much feared.

In the afternoon a couple of fishermen paddle into the bay in one of the dugout canoes and proceed to chum the water with bits of dead chicken and offal, but no one comes to fish. Strange, we think. That is, until 0530 the following morning, when there is a banging on *Nada*'s hull. A group of fishermen has rowed out an enormous net, suspended from floats and weighted with rocks at its base, clear across the mouth of the bay. Lines at each end run to the beach and the entire village has turned out to haul in the net. The fishermen are paddling slowly in front of the net, splashing the water to drive any fish toward the shore. We are in the middle. Not surprisingly, they are in a hurry for us to move: "Maintenant; maintenant (now; now)."

Chris and Liz, sleeping in the cockpit, emerge in pajamas and nightie. What a surreal sight this must have been for the fishermen! We hastily disassemble their bed, pull up our anchor, and motor slowly to one end of the net. A couple of fishermen hold down the hauling lines to let us over. It's just as well we have a full-keeled boat. Without it, the keel would snag the lines and foul up the whole operation: the last thing we need is to offend the entire village.

Since we are now up and going, we continue toward St. Lucia.

CHAPTER 7

ST. LUCIA, THE GRENADINES AND GRENADA

MAY TO JUNE 1987

BETWEEN FIERCE CARIB RESISTANCE, disease, and natural disaster, European invaders were unable to establish a permanent foothold on St. Lucia until a French expedition in 1643. Twenty years later the English seized the island but after two years the invasion force was reduced from 1,000 to 89, mostly through disease. The French regained control. Over the next 100 years, the island changed hands twelve times.

As on Guadeloupe, the French Revolution brought the guillotine for royalists and freedom for the slaves. The British, concerned that this would stir up the slaves on their islands, invaded. Freed slaves drove out the British together with every white slave owner. Their success, however, was short-lived; the British returned and restored slavery, although many of the rebels escaped into the rainforests that cloak St. Lucia's mountainous backbone. The British were not to grant full freedom to the slaves until 1838. St. Lucia finally became an independent nation in 1979.

It's a short sail from Martinique to St. Lucia. In all we cover a little over 30 miles on a close reach before anchoring in the totally protected lagoon at Rodney Bay on the west coast. Customs here are fast and friendly.

In the evening we dinghy to the beach and watch the sun set, and then make our way up the lagoon looking for a place to eat. The phosphorescence in the

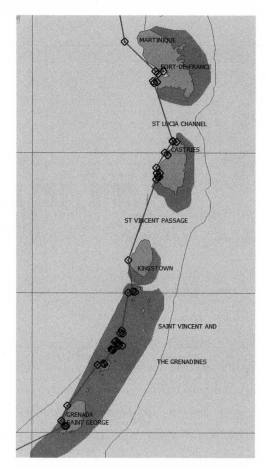

water is astonishing. The dinghy wake and outboard motor turbulence create a sensation of being in a swimming pool with blue underwater lighting. Fish darting away leave a zigzag wake. Sometimes a whole school of fish scatters in different directions, setting off an underwater fireworks display. It is a remarkable experience; we putter around for ages, food forgotten.

The following morning we move south around to Castries, the capital of St. Lucia, to go shopping. St. Lucia is one of those islands with a considerable amount of low-level hustling. As soon as the dinghy touches the dock in Castries a group of young boys are pushing and shoving, demanding to be the "watcher" while the crew is ashore. A watcher is a very necessary thing or the dinghy is just as likely to be cut loose.

Some cruisers become upset with this protection racket and get themselves into trouble. We don't mind: when we see the level of unemployment and the men hanging around on street corners all day, it is hard to blame anyone for trying to extract a dollar from yachties. We find the crowd is always good humored. We soon learn to pick out a particular boy, to ask his name, and to designate him as the watcher. On our return two or three invariably claim to have been watching the dinghy for us, but we pay our authorized watcher and leave him to sort it out with the others. There is no way we are going to arbitrate their disputes.

We find Castries is a lively West Indian town with excellent shopping. St. Lucia is a member of the British Commonwealth. We come across numerous tasty British products and stock up on Marmite, Branston Pickle and tea before heading south again to Marigot Bay. Here an inlet between rocky cliffs, barely visible from out at sea, leads past a coconut palmed sandy spit into a circular lagoon lined with mangroves and surrounded by verdant, coconut-covered hills on all sides. The holding is good, and the bay calm and protected. That evening we dine in the cockpit in the center of this striking natural amphitheater on roast lamb, roast potatoes, cauliflower with cheese sauce, and pineapple in Cointreau (a French liqueur) for dessert. Delicious.

Seven miles to the south of us lies Soufriere, the second largest town on St. Lucia, nestled along the shoreline at the foot of a barely active volcano. There is no decent anchorage here since the water is deep all the way into the shore. The cruising guides recommend tying to the jetty but we prefer peace and quiet and instead decide to anchor off the Hummingbird restaurant in the northeast corner of the bay.

On our approach we are met a mile or so out to sea by enterprising hustlers in a dugout canoe insisting on taking our line ashore. Ignoring our protestations, they follow us in. Close to the beach we throw out a stern anchor on a long rode. As the seabed rises to greet us, the anchor bites. We set it hard and ease on in toward the beach, handing our bow line to the hustler who has now run ashore. He ties us off to a coconut tree. As in Castries, we think it better to play the game rather than run the risk of being cut loose in the night.

We like Soufriere, although for some reason we have met few people who share this opinion. A fire destroyed the northern end of the town in 1955 and the new buildings are uninteresting, but the southern half of town is very West Indian with numerous charming homes decorated with fancy woodwork. The bay sweeps around to the dramatic peak of Petit Piton, an old volcanic cone, thrusting up almost 2,500 feet. Fishing folks' shacks line the narrow beach, clinging to the foot of the mountain. The fishing canoes, painted a mass of bright colors, are lined up along the shore, pointing out to sea. We see boats named *I Do Not Let Difficulties Interfere With My Aims*, *I Believe In One God*, and *Ghost Busters*.

In the mornings the fishermen paddle out in their canoes to string long nets across the bay. Because of the tremendous drop off it is quite impossible to reach the bottom—the nets merely skim the surface. The nets are drawn around in a wide arc and hauled in; periodically one of the guys dives in to see if they have anything. It is hard work and as often as not they come up empty handed, but with Petit Piton as a backdrop it certainly is photogenic. Fishermen coming in with their catch announce their arrival by blowing a conch horn and marching into town with the fish and a set of scales.

A steep road out of town leads to the volcano, a short bus ride away. Some of the buses are elaborately decorated old trucks. Terrie, Pippin, and I always enjoy our rides but Chris and Liz, having missed their basic training on guaguas, cannot relax crammed in the back of an old truck on mountain roads with a dozen other sweaty bodies.

The volcano is touted as "the only walk-in volcano in the world" but to call it a volcano at all is an optimistic use of language. What we are looking at is nothing more than a blow hole that has formed an eerie moonscape with cauldrons of boiling mud, steam issuing from the earth, little geysers, and the omnipresent stench of sulfur.

We walk back down to Soufriere through hillsides covered with coconut plantations. We come upon a farmer leading a couple of cows. Pippin is excited by any animal and like a typical father I pull out my camera to take a shot of her bouncing up and down in her backpack. The farmer is obviously immensely proud of these cows for he immediately assumes I want to take their picture! I can't disappoint him and so we wait while he arranges them to best effect and then I take a snapshot—would anyone like a photo of two St. Lucia cows?

Every sundown at Soufriere the bay, the town, and the mountains behind are lit in red. As the sun sinks lower and the light fades the windows in the shacks along the beach are afire with the last orange glow. And then the sun is gone over the horizon and it is time to look out to sea as the western sky lights up in a glorious tropical sunset. Finally the kaleidoscope of color fades into the night.

It is Sunday, May 10: departure day for Chris and Liz. They have an evening flight and we still have not been to the famous Pitons around the corner. Early in the morning we motor past the base of Petit Piton (2,425 feet high) toward the higher Gros Piton (2,579 feet). Between the two is a bay with the most dramatic anchorage in the Caribbean, the mountains rising near vertically on both sides with a beach and coconut plantation at the head of the bay. And there, wandering up and down the beach, is an elephant!

We are told that Idi Amin sent the elephant, Bupa, over as a baby from Uganda on a banana boat, and that it was set loose on this beach and stayed. This turns out to not be true—Bupa belongs to an eccentric British aristocrat, Colin Tennant, 3rd Baron Glenconner, owner of the island of Mustique in the Grenadines and of this bay, and intermittent host to an extraordinary ensemble of British royalty and rock stars, including Princess Margaret (sister of Queen Elizabeth II), Mick Jagger, and David Bowie. Subsequently, the elephant was rumored to have killed a tourist and been shot, but this also turns out to not be true—it choked to death. A Hilton Hotel now dominates the bay and has forever ruined it. When he died Lord Glenconner shocked the British establishment by leaving his St. Lucia estates to his manservant instead of his heirs.

As at Soufriere, we drop a stern anchor as we come slowly in to shore, trailing the anchor behind us until the seabed abruptly rises from the depths and the anchor bites. One of the local boys takes a bow line and ties us off to a tree.

On another occasion, for reasons I can't remember, we take a stern line ashore and I decide to row out the bow anchor into deep water. We load the 45 lb. CQR and 120 feet of chain into the dinghy. I row away from *Nada*, allowing the chain to run out over the dinghy's gunwale, controlling the rate at which it deploys with my foot. In no time at all I am in deep water with a considerable weight of chain hanging down. I lose control of the chain in the dinghy. It flies overboard in a rush with the last of it whipping the anchor across the dinghy as I scramble out of the way. The pointed fluke of the anchor smashes a hole in the side of the dinghy and jams there. The weight of the chain and anchor flip the dinghy on its side. The only thing that stops it going to the bottom is a considerable amount of foamed-in buoyancy. It takes a major effort (and a fair old backache) to pry the anchor loose and free the dinghy.

In any event, the snorkeling under the cliffs at the foot of Petit Piton makes the effort to get there worthwhile. Here for the first time we come across a school of squid, shimmering in iridescent colors. In the afternoon we take a guide and a local dugout canoe around Petit Piton to a landing spot at the base of a steep trail leading to a steaming waterfall issuing from the volcano. We have the most wonderful hot shower, pummeled and massaged by the cascading water. Subsequently we are warned that it is not safe to bathe in any of the freshwater streams in St. Lucia since all contain a dangerous parasite, but perhaps this close to the volcano the water is sterilized; we are OK.

We return to the landing spot to find our taxi canoe is nowhere to be seen. Messages relayed via passing boats bring back the news that he has pulled up out of the water and is finished for the day. This is typical of life in the islands and normally not a problem but today we are governed by an airline schedule. There are now only one or two canoes remaining. One of the last to leave, carrying a boatload of people to Soufriere, agrees to come back and get us; we wait anxiously on the beach wondering if he too will decide to quit for the day. But he shows up and ferries us back to *Nada*. We hurriedly untie from our tree, pull up the stern anchor, and motor back to our previous anchorage in front of the Hummingbird restaurant.

The airport is at the southern end of the island. We have already negotiated a price and arranged for a taxi to meet us at the Hummingbird; we still have time for a delicious meal. The taxi shows up as arranged, somewhat to our surprise, and then takes off as Chris and Liz gather their things and prepare to leave. We have another anxious wait, but just as we are getting really concerned he returns—he has gone to a hotel down the road to drum up additional business. Chris and Liz get away on time.

Back on *Nada*, our boat feels empty, and we are seized by a sense of loneliness and isolation. But on the other hand it is pleasing to have the space once again and a couple of clear berths. For a week or so we potter between Soufriere, Marigot Bay, and Castries while I write and Terrie paints. We are, in any case, unable to go anywhere since at some point I have banged my elbow and it has now developed a painful abscess, putting my arm out of commission. It is not healing, so I see a doctor who prescribes a course of antibiotics and in a few days it settles down. Terrie joins me in the doctor's office; she is becoming decidedly pregnant and the doctor gives us a due date for the end of July.

Pippin is growing fast. In my log I note: "She has very few words but understands a lot. Basically, she can say 'DaDa' and 'Fish.' Every time she sees a dog (or any animal for that matter) she barks excitedly. She must have been dreaming about dogs as she woke up from her midday nap barking."

She is now adamant about feeding herself. I'm sure all parents remember the experience. Somehow or another the spoon always turns over before it reaches the mouth. We have a disastrous morning when I make her oatmeal too thin and it keeps falling off the spoon. Oh, the wailing and temper tantrums, but no one is allowed to help. Breakfast is a very noisy and messy affair with no one satisfied. After that the oatmeal is thick enough to stick to a greased spoon.

We have additional food problems: we have imported weevils with recently bought brown rice. These have drilled through the packages and spread rapidly. We have to dump all our rice and spaghetti over the side.

We try to take Pippin swimming every day and to find a beach on which to play for an hour or two. In Castries we discover a fine one on the other side of Vigie airport, which abuts the anchorage. This must be the only airfield in the world where a public footpath crosses the main runway; when all is clear a green light is displayed in the control tower.

We are hearing more and more good reports of Venezuela from north-bound yachts. Friendly, uncrowded cruising, and unbelievably cheap. We have been thinking of having the baby in Grenada, an English speaking country, or perhaps leaving the boat there and flying back to the States, but Venezuela seems increasingly alluring. In anticipation of affordable restocking we begin to eat down our supplies without replacing them and over the next few weeks *Nada*'s waterline creeps imperceptibly upward.

Terrie writes to her sister: "Our future on the boat is up in the air. Nigel's back has really been plaguing him. He's afraid he might do long term damage with all the anchor winching and hauling up sails. He's afraid I might miscarry if I try doing it. We are thinking of trying to find someone young and strong to do this work… The thought of giving this up breaks my heart and it must really bother him too—to realize that physically you can't do what you've mentally and financially psyched yourself up to. There's so much more of the world I want to see. I think we've pretty much given up the idea of the Pacific. Some of the crossings are 15 days between islands and with two babies it just seems like too much. We are close to Venezuela now and have heard nothing but good reports about it and I wouldn't mind having the baby there…reckon it won't come until late July or August but really have no idea."

The Venezuelans, fortuitously, have a consulate by Vigie airport. We sail back to Castries and obtain visas in preparation; a good move, as it turns out, since the visas are issued almost immediately whereas we later meet sailors who had all kinds of problems elsewhere. Our visit coincides with a heavy rain that washes all the garbage out of Castries— "a disgusting mess of bottles, cans, plastic bags, and assorted rubbish." We foul the outboard motor propeller half a dozen times going into town and back.

With Terrie now almost seven months pregnant we need to get moving. St. Lucia is another turning point in the island chain; in optimistic expectation of some broad reaching and running I unfreeze the end fittings on our downwind poles, which have seen no action for some time. We have two poles which enable us to set two sails forward of the mast when running downwind. This creates a large sail area that is easily managed and de-powered, and as such is not likely to get us into trouble with unexpected wind shifts or when hit by a sudden squall.

* * * * *

Between St. Lucia and Grenada lie St. Vincent and the Grenadines, the latter being an archipelago of numerous small islands.

St. Vincent was one of the last of the Caribbean islands to be settled and subdued by the invading Europeans. The Carib indians put up a tough and prolonged resistance which was not completely broken until 1796, with several thousand being deported by the British to the island of Roatan off the Honduran coast (where there are still more-or-less isolated communities of their descendants). In 1987 St. Vincent has a reputation for crime against cruising sailors. We give it a miss and instead continue on to the Grenadines.

In just a few days we touch on half a dozen islands—Bequia, Canouan, Mayreau, the Tobago Cays, Union Island, and Carriacou. Each has its own personality.

Admiralty Bay, on the east side of Bequia, is one of the safest harbors in the eastern Caribbean for larger sailing ships. As such, it became a repair base for various navies and pirates, including, according to legend, the likes of Sir Francis Drake, Edward Teach (Blackbeard), and Henry Morgan. The island is still renowned as a center for wooden boatbuilding and fearless seamen. The Bequians are one of the few peoples in the world legally allowed to hunt humpback whales using hand-thrown harpoons launched from open boats.

When we sail in there are a couple of boats under construction at the water's edge. These are seagoing plank-on-frame boats far removed from the Carib dugout canoes we have seen lately. The boats are built without plans, based on decades of custom and practice, from rough balks of timber.

During our stopover in Bequia it rains on and off with heavy squalls, the wind fairly whistling through the rigging, but the anchorage at Admiralty Bay remains calm. We weave around our anchor chain dragging the slack across the rocky bottom. The noise is picked up and amplified by the hull: at night in the focs'l, where Terrie and I sleep, it sounds awful. We finally move into the main saloon for some peace and quiet. In spite of no wave action, we break the anchor snubbing line twice. I replace the ⅜-inch nylon line with ½-inch line.

We take Pippin swimming on beautiful Princess Margaret Beach and meet a couple who have sailed directly to Bequia from Ponce on the southern coast of Puerto Rico in eighty hours, reaching in comfort the whole way. This is about as much sailing time as we spent beating and motorsailing from the Virgin Islands to Antigua. It becomes clear to me that a correct strategy for seeing these islands is to sail direct to Grenada, or one of the southern islands, and to then work back up the island chain.

After Bequia the next stop is Canouan. "Hard on the wind almost all the way; choppy seas to begin with, taking more water over the deck than at any time on this whole trip. I was really pissed off! Ended up motorsailing with just the jib up. Toward Canouan seas built and lengthened into a decent swell, and came more on the beam—got a lot more comfortable. Anchored in Admiralty Bay, two anchors, and then wind swung around with tide from other direction, boats moving around, put us rather close to a charter boat (30 feet). They were obviously a little worried. They were on rope, we on chain and rope, different boats, etc.—we kept swinging around across their bow. I was reluctant to pull up anchors because of back and arm problems, but then couldn't sleep properly plus a heavy squall in the night. All in all, I am ready to get off the boat for a few months."

And then: "Sailed (yes, sailed!) to Mayreau (all of 4 miles). Very pleasant beam reach."

Salt Whistle Bay on the northwestern tip of Mayreau gives us a pro-tected anchorage overlooking a sandy beach and coconut plantation. A footpath leads through thickets of thorn to the top of the island; from here we can see clear down to Grenada in the south, and up to Bequia in the north, and every island in between.

Mayreau, with its one small settlement, is as poor as any island we have seen. There are no hedges or fences; the vegetation is scrubby with a lot of cactus and thorn. Chickens, turkeys, dogs, goats and pigs are running loose with naked children. Only two houses have electricity, sharing the same generator; there are no roads and no cars. The previous year the Canadian government had paid to cement the footpaths around town, and we feel this is an outstanding example of effective foreign aid. In place of a large project, many of which generate corruption and ultimately fail, this small labor intensive investment provided work for a while and significantly improved the lot of everyone on the island: when it rains the people no longer have to slip and slide down steep, muddy hillsides.

From Mayreau we sail the short distance to the picture-perfect Tobago Cays. We anchor behind World's End Reef, highly regarded by Jacques Cousteau. Unfortunately, one squall after another sweeps over us, roiling the waters and limiting the snorkeling, and the sun never breaks through the cloud cover the entire time we are there.

* * * * *

A couple more islands, a couple more layovers, and here we are motorsailing in calm water down the lee side of Grenada toward St. George's. What a luxuriant island this is. Mountains draped in tropical rainforest drop precipitously into the sea, with every once in a while a beach of black volcanic sand tucked in at the foot of a valley. These valleys have been fought over with the same intensity, mayhem and misery as on most West Indian islands.

The British were the first to attempt a permanent settlement in 1609; the Caribs successfully drove them out. The French made a more determined effort beginning in 1649. It took five years to crush the Carib resistance, with the last of the defenders throwing themselves off a cliff rather than surrender. The British and French then fought over the island for the better part of 100 years, with intermittent slave rebellions and natural disasters, before the British consolidated their control. From the 1920s onward, faced with considerable anti-colonial local pressure, Britain gradually relinquished its control, until Grenada finally became a fully independent state.

Even in modern times Grenada has been ravaged by the struggles between great powers. In 1979 the New Jewel Movement, with Maurice Bishop at its head, seized power, establishing a single-party state with close ties to Cuba and other communist countries. With Cuban help Grenada began to build an airport with a runway long enough to handle international jets, ostensibly to boost its tourist industry. The U.S., paranoid that Grenada would become another client base for Russia in the cold war, saw the airfield as a major strategic threat.

A power struggle within the New Jewel Movement in 1983 between Bishop and hard-line Marxists, supported by the head of the army, resulted in the ousting and arrest of Bishop, who was executed along with other members of his cabinet. The army declared a four-day curfew and announced that anyone leaving his or her house would be shot on sight. Six days later, the U.S. Marines invaded, rapidly defeating the Grenadian army, and withdrawing shortly thereafter. Ironically, the Americans then helped to complete the airport. The coup leaders were found guilty of murder and sentenced to death, with the sentences later commuted to life. They are still in jail.

St. George's, the capital of Grenada, comes into sight, houses lining the steep hillsides, with still no sign of the harbor entrance shown on our chart. And then through a break in the coastline the harbor suddenly comes into view, high hills on both sides, rocks and cliffs to starboard with a bullet-scarred building on top, a legacy of the American invasion, and the old British Fort George to port, commanding the harbor and its approaches. As we sail in, the waterfront of St. George's (the Carenage) appears to the north, looking for all the world like some old European seaport.

The original wooden town was burnt to the ground in 1771 and again in 1775 after which it was rebuilt in brick and stone. Restored eighteenth century warehouses with red tiled roofs line the quayside. The bricks and tiles came over as ballast on sailing ships in days of old to be replaced by rocks and spices on the return voyage. During our stay, tied up alongside are almost always one or two inter-island trading sloops, now with engines, but still sporting masts and sails. The quayside is constantly alive with activity as the boats are loaded and unloaded by hand.

The harbor and lagoon occupy the remains of a drowned volcanic caldera. The harbor entrance is a break in the old volcano walls. The yacht anchorage is in the lagoon across the harbor to the south. Entrance is via a narrow dredged channel, well marked with buoys. Hills rise up on all sides, forming one of the most protected anchorages in this part of the Caribbean, which is one reason it has been so well fought over by the French and British. The stern and imposing walls of Fort George bear mute testimony to the passions of old.

To one side of the anchorage is a small meadow with sheep grazing and a wooden building that is the headquarters of a large steel band. Night after night we are entertained at anchor into the early hours of the morning as the band beats out its rhythms.

Although the anchorage is always calm, strong winds funnel through. The bottom is soft mud and we find two anchors are required to keep *Nada* from dragging. Wind shifts blow the boats around in circles, twisting up anchor rodes. When we finally leave, it takes us an hour to disentangle our two lines, wrapped tightly around one another.

A BAHAMIAN MOOR

When a second anchor is set astern, with both rodes coming back over the bow, this is known as a Bahamian moor (it gets this name because with both rodes tightened it significantly limits a boat's turning circle, enabling more boats to safely anchor in crowded Bahamian anchorages). The other place a Bahamian moor is very useful is when anchoring in an estuary with a strong tidal stream. When the current reverses it will stop the boat from swinging into the bank or out into the channel.

The normal way to execute a Bahamaian moor is to drop and set the first anchor in the usual manner, and then fall back at least double the necessary scope to drop the second anchor. The first rode is tightened until the boat is positioned midway between the two anchors, at which time tightening the rodes will set the second anchor as above.

Whatever is done, if the anchorage has a reversing current or tidal stream it is important to recognize that individual boats will respond to the change in current in different ways. Those with long keels and low freeboard will turn first as the current gets a hold on their underbodies, while those with fin keels and high freeboard will tend to be held in place by the wind. At times, the boats will be lying in completely different directions. If they are anchored too close to one another, they will collide.

When using nylon rodes in a reversing stream, with certain keel and rudder types (especially fin keels and spade rudders) there is a risk of fouling one of the rodes as the boat swings through 180 degrees. In this case, it is advisable to lower a weight down the rode that is streaming aft so that this rode is held down. Such a weight is known as a kellett; the line on which it is lowered is a sentinel. The use of a kellett with a nylon rode will also improve the holding power of most anchors.

At anchor we have awnings that we string from one end of *Nada* to the other, with a wind scoop that attaches to the underside of the awning and funnels air into the forward cabin where we sleep. If there is any kind of a breeze at all, it works just as well as air conditioning without the expense and energy demands. The arrangement is such that we can leave the wind scoop up even in a downpour. We have a couple of drain fittings installed at low spots in the sides of the awning. When it rains, we can funnel the water into jerry cans to top up our tanks; we almost never need to go on a dock to obtain water.

"Rain!" At 2 am Terrie and I scramble out naked in the middle of the crowded lagoon. Water is already cascading out of the awning's drain fittings. We grab a couple of jerry cans and set them in place. This is a regular cloudburst; both jerry cans are already overflowing. Terrie is bringing out buckets, the pressure cooker, and pots and pans. There is no sign of a let-up to the downpour so we abandon the pots, grab a couple of brushes, and scrub the starboard side decks where our water tank fills are situated. The decks are soon flushed of dirt and salt. We open the water tanks, plug the side deck drains, and in ten minutes the tanks are full to capacity (200 gallons). We have enough water for another 5 weeks cruising (we are very frugal).

Grenada is friendly, lively, and colorful with no hint of the recent strife. The land is rich and fertile and just about anything grows. The open market in St. George's displays a wide variety of fruits and vegetables. Extravagantly decorated buses take off from the market square for every part of the island; we are able to tour at almost no cost. All but the low-lying southern part of Grenada is covered in rich tropical jungle nourished by abundant rainfall; the higher areas of the island receive 160 inches a year. Dozens of streams cascade down the mountainsides the short distance to the sea. We bathe in a picture perfect pool at the foot of a waterfall. Everywhere the houses are neat and tidy, with well-kept hedges and flower gardens, the little villages set among acre after acre of banana plantations.

Grenada is the "Spice Island". Inland are large estates of nutmeg trees, and dotted around the hillsides are many individual nutmegs amongst the other trees. The farmers wait until the fruit is ripe and splits open. To avoid bruising, it is then picked before it falls to the ground. The fruit is cut away and used to make preserves; the kernel is shipped to Grenville.

Grenville, on the east coast, is the second city of Grenada, home to the nutmeg factory—a large wooden structure in which 260 people work. The fresh nutmeg kernels have a bright red outer layer of mace, inside which is the nutmeg itself. The mace is stripped off and laid out on large trays to dry, slowly turning bright yellow in the process. The nutmegs are graded by hand according to size and passed through a simple machine (the only machine in the whole factory) to crack the shell. The pieces of shell are picked off and the kernels laid on more trays to also dry. Later they are bagged and shipped out.

Years after we leave, Hurricane Ivan, a category 4 hurricane, makes a direct hit on Grenada, destroying most of the nutmeg crop along with 85% of the structures on the island.

We stay long enough in Grenada to have our mail forwarded to the post office. While we are waiting for it we move to the southern coast, which has excellent anchorages and beaches, though not nearly such striking scenery. The land is lower and dryer, with scrubby vegetation.

We learn how to cook breadfruit, the plant that got Captain Bligh into so much trouble. He was bringing it back to the West Indies as a source of starch for the slaves when his crew mutinied. The fruit is quite large—bigger than a grapefruit—and has a tough outer skin. It is placed directly on an open flame and rotated every once in a while until the whole skin is charcoaled. The skin is then picked off, leaving a vegetable something like a potato.

Back in St. George's we see Don Street's *Iolaire* in the harbor— "Altogether a little bit of a wreck considering it is the most famous boat in the Caribbean!" I dinghy over hoping for advice on writing and publishing but he has left for his home in Ireland. We treat ourselves to dinner at Mama's, a local institution. What a meal it is, with twenty-one dishes of superbly cooked West Indian delicacies: calalue soup for starters; green salad; breadfruit salad; lobster salad; lobster, crab, and breadfruit fritters; curried mutton; rice; pork; beef; pigs' trotters; turkey legs; tuna; manicou (possum); another crab dish; cornmeal and coconut; giant crawfish; fried plantains; green bananas; turtle; yams. Is that twenty-one? Somewhere along the line I have lost one. And then for dessert, the piéce de resistance: chocolate cake and coconut ice cream, washed down with a cup of tea (how very British). Mama, a fat jovial woman, plays with Pippin and then falls asleep in her chair.

Most days Terrie takes Pippin on the bus to swim and play on the white sand Grand Anse beach just out of town. They strike up a friendship with a Rastafarian woman with impressive dreadlocks. Whereas on some of the other islands Rastas can be quite hostile to white people, on Grenada they are always friendly. When we leave, the woman gives Terrie a finely embroidered vest and presents me with a pair of swimming trunks in the Rasta colors of green, orange, and purple.

Our mail arrives—two large boxes of it. What excitement! It is mid-June and Terrie is now almost eight months pregnant. Until this time, Terrie has been as fit as a fiddle and we have not given the birth a great deal of thought but now we are beginning to get apprehensive. I am brushing up on delivery procedures in case she goes into premature labor on the way to Venezuela. She rather likes the idea of having the baby in Venezuela, but I am not so keen on taking care of her and a newborn in the small confines of our boat, in a country in which neither of us speaks much of the language, and in the sometimes-stifling heat of a tropical summer. Besides which, our one-time vast stock of diapers is almost exhausted.

The closer we get to D-Day (Delivery Day) the more inclined I am to bail out and fly home to the States. I check on airline tickets and find they are prohibitively expensive from St. George's whereas from Caracas, the capital of Venezuela, they will be much less costly. We are told there is a cheap and secure marina at Cumana in northeast Venezuela where we can leave *Nada* in safety and that settles it. We need to make a move before Terrie's water breaks!

CHAPTER 8
VENEZUELA
JUNE AND OCTOBER–NOVEMBER 1987

WE LEAVE ST. GEORGE'S on Grenada in mid-afternoon for an overnight sail to Isla de Margarita, an island just off the Venezuelan mainland. At last we put the downwind poles to use, running almost dead before the wind, at times wing and wing, the current too pushing us on—during the night it gives us a 10-mile boost. Our autopilot, which has worked flawlessly for months, packs up, forcing us to hand steer the rest of the way to Venezuela. We sight Los Testigos, a group of islands owned by Venezuela, at dawn. The wind eases and I am unsure if we will be safely anchored at Isla de Margarita before nightfall. Rather than run the risk of having to heave-to all night off the island, awaiting dawn to enter, we layover at Los Testigos for the day and take off again that night. I needn't have worried; with the wind and current at our back we have to reduce sail to the staysail alone to hold our speed down and avoid closing Isla de Margarita in the dark. We are not used to this fast downwind sailing.

Columbus was here before us on his third voyage in 1498, naming this and the island of Cubagua, closer to the mainland, the "Pearl Islands" because of the abundant pearl oysters. By 1530 the indigenous population and oysters had both been devastated.

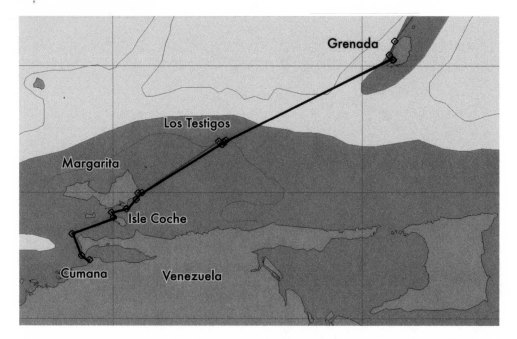

Pampatar on the east end of Isla de Margarita is the port of entry. The anchorage affords poor protection and is rolly. We dinghy ashore through a moderate surf. Three or four men rush forward to help Terrie and Pippin and to haul the dinghy up the beach. After months of being hustled in the West Indies we try to brush them off before we realize they aren't clamoring for a tip but just being helpful. What a refreshing change: a small gesture like this makes a big impression. But of course, this is a Hispanic country, and how good it feels to be back amongst spontaneously friendly people.

But then too we have to make our peace with the bureaucracy. This entails visits to the customs, the Guardia Civil, the immigration office, and finally the port captain, a long walk out of town in the hot sun, carrying Pippin the whole way. Everyone is very friendly and we are issued lots of paperwork with impressive stamps. When we leave we have to clear out with the same people (except immigration) in reverse order (this is important!) and then check in once again with their counterparts on the mainland.

Our supplies are getting a little short. We catch a bus to Porlamar, the capital of the island. Isla de Margarita is a free port with excellent shopping in Porlamar but without a doubt what sets every yachtie drooling are the supermarkets—as clean and well stocked as any in the States, but at half the prices. After months of lean and expensive pickings we run around like children let loose in a candy store—Terrie buys five cantaloupe melons! We are beginning to realize that Venezuela is at least as friendly and inexpensive as we have repeatedly been told, but scarcely believed.

We clear out and set sail south and west for Cumana, breaking our journey for a night behind a long sand spit on Isla Coche. We have a very poor chart of the area. I misjudge the approach to the spit; we hit the hard sandy bottom several times in the troughs of small waves before getting clear and rounding it. Friends are not so lucky. Sailing direct from St. Thomas to Grenada they first blow out their sails in heavy squalls, and then lose the oil from their transmission (due to a faulty repair job in St. Thomas) and seize the transmission. They drift for several days before being washed up in 3 feet of water on Isla Coche. Fortunately their boat suffers no damage but it takes seven local fishing boats to pull them off. They are towed into Cumana where the authorities give them a hard time for not having the proper paperwork!

The wind whistles across the sand spit keeping us cool with hardly a ripple on the surface of the water. The local fishermen clean their catch nearby, the small fry thrown out and washed up on the beach. This attracts thousands of birds—pelicans, cormorants, and several other species. In the evening the birds congregate on the sand and in the water around us. Pippin entertains herself by chasing flocks of birds up and down the beach.

One last fast downhill run, largely in sheltered water, sees us safely docked in the marina at Cumana. This is a fairly recent development, with shorepower and fresh water (what a luxury) in every slip, and an armed guard on the gate. Half a dozen guardia board us, make a thorough search, check our paperwork, and leave. I wrongly think we are cleared in and never realize my mistake until months later, which then causes us something of a headache.

The very first thing the following morning I head into town to book round-trip tickets to the States for flights departing in two weeks' time (to make sure

we are gone before the baby arrives), returning in October. This will give us time to recommission *Nada* by the time hurricane season ends in November.

* * * * *

The marina is a little out of town. A short walk connects with an excellent bus service. The walk, however, is past a shantytown of makeshift shacks and open sewers. A couple of yachties have been robbed although we never feel the least bit threatened, even at night. We always have Pippin with us in her backpack, and later Paul, and the minute we come by we are mobbed by a crowd of friendly and curious children who come dashing out of the slum, with Paul's red hair causing something of a sensation—everyone wants to touch it. Their parents wave cheerfully to us from open doorways. Children really are a magic talisman in Hispanic countries.

Cumana was the first permanent Spanish settlement in Venezuela, established around 1520. Ironically, one of the initial waves of explorer-settlers was German, given a license to search for the golden city of El Dorado in return for canceling debts owed by Charles I of Spain. Thereafter, colonization of Venezuela was a relatively slow affair, with the chief economic activity being the raising of livestock and subsequently extending to cocoa plantations worked by African slaves. Cocoa became the principal export.

The original town of Cumana was destroyed several times by successful native attacks. It was reconstructed in 1569, but almost totally destroyed by earthquakes in 1766 and 1797. None of the town we find is really old, but nevertheless there are a number of fine buildings, in particular the cathedral with an elaborately ornate interior, and the seventeenth-century fort that has been fully restored. The town is built on both banks of the Manzanares river, with an attractive small park in the city center.

In a letter Terrie writes home: "First day to walk around Venezuela. Very hot, so we drank many batidos. Ordered 'dos batidos y tres aguas' and got two batidos and three ham and cheese sandwiches ('saguas'). Later, ordered 'dos batidos con leche' and received two delicious coffees! We were on the church steps, Nigel throwing an empty juice carton up a few steps to Pippin.

She was getting pretty good at throwing it back until she got so enthusiastic she threw one so hard she did a somersault down a couple of steps. That was the end of that game." Overshadowing everything, at least in Terrie's mind, is the El Bariloche ice cream parlor with the most sumptuous banana splits ever devised (Banana Manias) that cost 60 cents each.

As elsewhere in the Caribbean, the French Revolution followed by the Napoleonic Wars, during which Napoleon took over Spain, appointing his own brother as king, lit the fuse of independence in Venezuela and neighboring Colombia. The First Republic was declared in 1811 but defeated the following year. Simon Bolivar led a renewed uprising that established the Second Republic in 1813 but this too was crushed. A third war resulted in independence from Spain in 1821. Bolivar fell out with his compatriots. The country has been plagued by the power struggles between successive strongmen for most of its subsequent history.

The first government elected with universal suffrage in 1947 was overthrown by a bloodless coup the following year, ushering in ten years of military dictatorship. A succession of nominally democratic governments then successfully faced down minor insurrections from the right and the left. The dramatic rise in the price of oil initiated by the 1972 Arab oil embargo provided Venezuelan regimes with a massive new source of income which was spent with enthusiasm and used as collateral to rack up huge foreign debts.

Venezuela in the summer of 1987 is a wonderful place for Americans to visit. In an attempt to halt runaway inflation, the government controls all prices. The Bolivar, the Venezuelan currency, is falling rapidly against the dollar on the foreign exchange markets without any equivalent adjustment of internal prices. This makes everything unbelievably cheap. It also makes it possible for us to travel all over the country, staying in hotels, for almost nothing. We decide to make the most of our two weeks before flying out.

We go to Guayachero near Caripe, to the east. Here a series of caves lead underground for miles. Guides take tourists in with kerosene lanterns casting a feeble glow; we join a party of about six. After the first few caves we are surrounded by pitch black, the entrance long since out of sight. There are many large birds that fly past in the dark and make an eerie noise in the recesses of the caves. About a mile in we have to squeeze through a narrow passage with a couple of bends. The guide goes ahead to light the way but as he turns the corners the rest of us are in near total darkness. One of the women in the party panics and becomes quite hysterical. For a while she will go neither forward nor backward but then allows a couple of friends to help her out. We all turn back. We are not sure whether or not we enjoyed the experience.

We catch an early morning bus to Ciudad Bolivar, a large inland city on the Orinoco river—a tiring all-day ride down mostly poor roads. Ciudad Bolivar is another old and historic city, founded in 1595. It later became Simon Bolivar's provisional capital (1817–1819) in his epic struggle for independence. The outskirts of the city are heavily industrialized, but the city center contains a number of fine old Spanish colonial buildings. For us it is a jumping off point for Canaima.

Canaima is a Venezuelan national park and the site of the Angel Falls, the highest waterfall in the world (3,000 feet). It is in a rugged inaccessible area south of the Orinoco river, peopled mostly by still primitive Indians. AVENSA, the Venezuelan national airline, has a landing strip close by that is long enough to accommodate a Boeing 727. Nearby is a chalet-style hotel alongside another tremendous waterfall (the Hacha Falls on the Caroni river). For $150 the three of us fly there and back and stay two nights and three days in the hotel, including all our meals. We take a trip in a giant dugout canoe—60 feet long and 5 feet wide, hollowed out of a single log—down the river through thick jungle to another small waterfall in which we bathe. Later we circle in the thundering spray and swirling whirlpools of foam at the foot of the Hacha Falls.

The next day we sneak out of the hotel and follow a trail through the jungle up the side of the Hacha Falls (such unsupervised trips are frowned on by the guardia who like to keep everyone under control). Above the falls we come upon an Indian family fishing. They have crossed the turbulent river in a tiny dugout canoe from their stick-and-palm-thatch settlement, hacked out of the jungle on the far side. The parents are fishing while a naked baby daughter sits in a giant leaf, its spine acting as a drain in place of a diaper, chewing on some plant. She seems to be stoned out of her head—Pippin tries without success to penetrate her glazed mind.

In a clearing another group are chopping away with adzes at an enormous tree, building one of the dugout canoes. The freeboard of the hollowed out log is being increased by adding a single plank on each side, the same technique we have seen from Martinique only on a much grander scale. The workers tell us they can build a canoe in a week, which we find mind-boggling until one of them saunters over to a small palm-thatched hut and comes out with a large chainsaw. A few minutes later another comes trotting up the trail carrying a six-pack of Coke: the twentieth century meets the Iron Age.

The topography here is fascinating. As soon as we climb up out of the immediate river valley the jungle gives way to open grassland and stunted trees (the Gran Sabana). Some mineral in the soil (tannin, I believe) prevents the jungle from taking root in spite of the heavy rainfall and near equatorial conditions. The same mineral gives the Caroni river a most unusual reddish-brown color. In the background are enormous shear-sided, flat-topped, rocky mesas, known locally as tepuis, which rise thousands of feet straight into the clouds. The tallest, Roraima, is over 9,000 feet high. Many have never been explored.

The Angel Falls are a rough, five-day canoe trip from the hotel site. We are not permitted to go with Pippin (the guardia again). Nevertheless, we still get a close look. When we fly out the pilot of our 727 takes us up the Angel Falls canyon, with the clouds low enough to block out the canyon rim above us. He flies first a tight right-handed and then a left-handed donut inside the canyon below the clouds, so that everyone can view the falls. The passengers are encouraged to scramble from one side of the plane to the other to have a second look! It's chaotic and scary as the wing tips pass just a few hundred feet from the cliff faces. The pilot then heads up into the clouds skimming over the top of the canyon wall.

On the return bus ride from Ciudad Bolivar we come up against the guardia again. They seem to intrude into every facet of Venezuelan life. On all the major highways there are periodic roadblocks, with most cars being stopped and searched, and papers checked. On this occasion the bus is pulled over and boarded by the guardia, who proceed to make a speech. One of them then displays a box of drinking glasses that they are selling for some fundraiser. We find the incident bizarre to the point of being comical but refrain from smiling. No one else is displaying any amusement and the glasses rapidly sell out. You don't mess with the guardia.

Back on *Nada* we spend a last couple of days cleaning and vacuuming; putting down roach poison; doubling up the docking lines; tying in lengths of chain in place of the lines wherever they lead across the dock and may chafe; closing the seacocks; and tightening the stuffing box that seals the entry point of the propeller shaft into *Nada* to eliminate any drips. We have no electric bilge pump, preferring to rely on high-capacity manual pumps when we are aboard, and so I am always a little apprehensive at any potentially long stay away from *Nada*—as little as a steady drip will eventually sink her.

We make Terrie's belly as inconspicuous as we can, fearful the airline will not let us board the plane, and fly back to New Orleans on June 30.

* * * * *

We stay long enough in Louisiana to say hello to friends and relatives and then drive 37 hours nonstop to the mountains in Montana to beat the heat and humidity. We stay with Terrie's sister, Laura, and her husband Ron, who own a family farm in the Clark's Fork Valley close to the Beartooth Mountains. Passing through Colorado on the way north, Pippin at one point wakes to her first sight of the Rockies. "Look, Mommy," she says, "islands without water."

We slip in a couple of fishing sorties at 10,000 feet among the alpine lakes of the Beartooth Mountains followed by a hike up Clark's Fork Canyon in search of mountain goats. By now Terrie is just a few days from her predicted due date and I am getting a little anxious about these off-road trips. "Dear Mum and Dad, the baby is due any day, perhaps any hour. We managed to get in a little last minute trout fishing up in the mountains over the past few days, but kept reasonably close to the road in case we had to beat a hasty retreat! Our little tent is getting crowded with the three of us—I don't think it will handle four. The fishing was excellent as usual. Terrie is doing fine and is as fit as a fiddle, climbing up and down hills with Pippin on her back half the time."

A day or two later Terrie goes into labor. Unlike the protracted labor when Pippin was born (which finally reduced Terrie to yelling, "I don't care what the fuck you do; you can cut me or drug me, just get it out!" She did, however, hang in there long enough to have a natural birth) the birth is fast and relatively painless—Terrie is in and out of the hospital in Red Lodge in six hours. I think they find us rather eccentric: Terrie insists on taking the placenta home on the theory that if it has nurtured a baby it will make good fertilizer. It is handed to us as we leave in a plastic supermarket shopping bag. We bury it at the foot of a raspberry bush in her sister's garden (the raspberries have never done too well; so much for that theory).

"Dear Mum and Dad, Terrie and Paul Norman Orion are doing well. We were in and out of the hospital so quickly that the accounts department called me up and said they didn't know how to bill us since no one had come and gone so quickly before! The first afternoon home Pippin thought Paul was an exciting new toy. By the next day she clearly thought it was nice to have seen him but it was time for him to leave. I turned my back for two seconds and she dragged him off the sofa by one leg and dropped him on the floor! The next day she was hitting him with the flyswatter! However, all in all the biggest problem is likely to be her being over affectionate as she gets carried away and smothers him with kisses from time to time. We managed to get in a little camping and fishing in the mountains just before Paul was born. The trout were as good as ever. We were planning to go back up the day Terrie went into labor since all the old ladies around here had decided she had another week to go!"

From Terrie: "Dear Mum and Pops, well, what do you know, we are doing it all over again. I really didn't want another but Nigel wisely thought it was only fair to Pippin and already she's taken to him and although she needs a lot of watching soon they will play together—hopefully."

Our stay in the States is rewarding in other ways. I am able to complete the publication process for *Repairs at Sea* and sign a contract to produce another book the following year. The new one is to be a substantial work on maintenance of boat equipment (it becomes the *Boatowner's Mechanical and Electrical Manual*). I set about contacting dozens and dozens (eventually hundreds) of boat equipment manufacturers in search of technical information, manuals, and troubleshooting guides, all of which will be impossible to come by once we are back on *Nada*.

It is beginning to look as if I may be able to make a sufficient living as a marine writer to support cruising indefinitely, albeit on a severely limited budget. To make this possible we are extremely frugal, staying with relatives or living in cheap rented accommodations when ashore, buying all our clothes from thrift stores or yard sales, and rarely eating out or spending anything on entertainment. Pretty much every spare penny we have ever generated has gone into *Nada*. We prefer to live the life we choose to live, and to scale back our needs by whatever is necessary to do this, rather than to live to fund the material things that others seem to find so essential.

We have no health insurance, which is a significant concern now that we have two children. However, we are all healthy and we feel the risk is worth taking. Instead, for the next several years we struggle to set aside a sum of money each year to give us a cushion in case any of us get sick. This ultimately becomes the down payment on the first house we buy four years later.

In the interim, we rely heavily on my twice-yearly royalty checks (at the end of September and March) from International Marine, supplemented with an increasing success rate in terms of selling articles to magazines. For the better part of a decade we are always broke by November. In order to save money, we take off for the Caribbean on *Nada* as soon as hurricane season is ended, sailing at least until the next royalty check arrives in late March. So long as we stay out of marinas, living on board is considerably cheaper than living ashore.

This year, before returning to *Nada* we hike back into the Beartooth Mountains for another fishing trip with Paul strapped to one or other of our chests as we cast into the lakes and streams. Terrie gives Pippin a brook trout to play with which keeps her amused as it wriggles through her fingers. I sense that things have gone quiet behind us. I turn around and all I can see of Pippin is two legs and a diaper sticking out of the ground. She has chased the fish into a water-filled hole the same diameter as her body and is stuck with her head and upper body submerged. If I had not seen her she would have drowned within the next couple of minutes. Considerably shaken, I pull her out by the feet. She is none the worse for the dunking but upset at the loss of the fish; from then on she is never out of sight.

We drive back to Louisiana with the two babies to catch our return flight to Venezuela. Terrie writes my parents: "Dear Mum and Dad, we fly down to Venezuela the first week in October to resume our travels… Pippin has really settled down just fine, though she has to be watched as she still tries to pick him (Paul) up and haul him around. Just yesterday we heard this big thump— she had carried him out the back room in the house and dropped him on the hard wood floor in the hall!"

Ten weeks to the day after Paul's birth we fly into Caracas loaded down with two huge cardboard boxes stuffed with boat equipment manuals and 500 disposable diapers. Added to this are a very large hold-all; a rucksack; a portable baby bed; extensive camera gear; three carry-on bags; Pippin's backpack; and of course Pippin and Paul. The whole lot, excluding Pippin and Paul, weighs 300 pounds. The Venezuelan customs insist on taking out and inspecting everything. What a mess. It is early evening by the time we are cleared and we have an 0600 flight to Cumana. Rather than try and drag everything to a hotel and then have to get up and find a taxi at 0430, we move to a corner of the departures hall, make a mattress out of the diapers, and bed down for the night in the airport. I don't suppose they see this too often! Caracas airport has stone floors; it is a hard and uncomfortable night.

The closer we get to *Nada* the more apprehensive I become. After three and a half months what will we find? What if she has been taking on water? I needn't have worried: there is dust in the bilges as usual. Everything is in fine shape though a little swelled up—hinges, engine controls, etc. Weevils, however, have hatched out in the dry goods and run riot throughout the boat.

While I set to work greasing and running up equipment, Terrie dumps our flour and pastas overboard, cleans out lockers, and hunts down strays.

We have bought some close-meshed netting in the States and spend the next couple of days installing this around the lifelines, trying to make them childproof. The first thing Pippin does is climb the net: we have to make this a very severe (spanking) offense (just as previously she has been confined to the cockpit at sea, and not allowed to hang through the lifelines in port or at anchor). We are having problems finding a home for all the gear we have brought with us, the diapers in particular taking up a lot of space, and *Nada* is a mess. Terrie and I are arguing about cleaning up and putting things away: it is just like old times!

Terrie gets a little light relief with a night out at the ballet. "Dear Mum and Pops… Paul and I went to a ballet in the castle at the top of the hill last night. Nigel gladly stayed with Pippin as he is no ballet or opera lover. I went with several other ladies whose husbands were of a similar inclination. There was a pleasant breeze that gently blew the ladies' dresses, creating a very feminine effect, and they had soldiers dressed as in the Nutcracker suite guarding the gates and turrets. Very elegant. We walked to the ice cream parlor in the mild evening weather… Paul is a good baby—wish I could say the same for Pippin! She's heading into her terrible twos with both guns blazing. Everything is 'No, No, No.' Even when she's playing by herself she'll murmur 'No, No, No' just to keep in practice!" I note in my log: "Pippin started teething again after a nice peaceful two or three months. False alarm! Just being difficult."

* * * * *

Our plan is to cruise through Venezuela's offshore islands—Tortuga, Los Roques, and Las Aves—about which we have been receiving rave reviews, before touching upon the Dutch ABC islands (Aruba, Bonaire, and Curacao) en route to the San Blas archipelago off the coast of Panama. We have reluctantly decided to give Colombia a miss—the few first-hand reports that we have received are not reassuring: too much drug money, random crime, and corruption.

The San Blas Islands, home to the Cuna Indians, are our primary goal. The Cuna, the second smallest race on earth after the Pygmies, are reputed to have a unique matriarchal society; when men marry they move into the bride's home. The women control the money and until recently coconuts have been the currency. The Cuna women are said to be lavishly decorated with gold ornaments, wearing the most beautiful molas— blouses sewn from multiple layers of brightly colored cloth which are cut away to create colorful images, the whole handstitched with exquisitely small stitches.

While in the States I have done a little research. The Cuna are fiercely independent and still racially and culturally pure to a degree long since lost by most South American indians. Until the 1940s children of Cuna women begot through mixing with non-Cuna men were killed at birth. Panama, the formal ruler, attempted to assert its sovereignty in the 1920s by sending over a squad of police, all of whom were murdered. Since then the Cuna have been left largely to their own devices.

All that is changing. The Peace Corps, in a misguided attempt to be helpful, introduced sewing machines to the San Blas Islands in the 1960s thinking this would turn mola making into a cottage industry but instead at a stroke it devalued the artistic integrity of the mola. A weekly cruise ship is now visiting the capital of the San Blas Islands, and Western influence is rapidly spreading and undermining the indigenous culture. So, for many reasons we are in a hurry to reach the San Blas and to spend time in the out islands where the old culture will still be most intact.

Although so close to the Panama Canal, the gateway to the South Pacific, I have finally reconciled myself to abandoning the round-the-world cruise. Terrie doesn't really care either way, so long as we minimize the passages and maximize the time spent in exotic places; the Pacific was always my dream. From the San Blas we intend to sail in leisurely fashion up the Caribbean coast of Central America—Panama, Costa Rica, Nicaragua (if it seems safe), Honduras, Guatemala, Belize, the Yucatan—and so finally back to New Orleans across the Gulf of Mexico.

Our departure, however, has to wait. Close to the marina in Cumana is a yard with a marine railway. We decide to haul *Nada* and renew our anti-fouling paint. The yard is fully booked for a while so we take off to see some more of Venezuela, catching a plane to Merida in the Andes.

Merida is another ancient city, founded in 1558, centered in the Venezuelan Andes and nestling in a long valley at an elevation of 5,000 feet. The mountains behind the city rise to over 16,000 feet with the world's longest and highest cable car running to the top in four stages (the cable car was closed in 2008 and has not yet reopened). At the summit we find there is still snow on the ground, despite being within a few hundred miles of the equator. Lugging Pippin and Paul around at this high of an altitude, we find ourselves rapidly out of breath.

On the way down, at the third landing stage, around 12,000 feet, Terrie discovers mules can be ridden for a dozen miles down steep mountain trails to the village of Los Nevados. She desperately wants to go but I balk at the idea. I am like a sack of potatoes on a horse (or mule) and Paul seems a little too young (at eleven weeks) for such an adventure in the high Andes. We have all kinds of tears ("Oh how I cried!" she writes), and so against my better judgment, I give in but much to my relief the mule drivers refuse to take us. Instead we go back down the way we came up, rent a car, and drive into the mountains.

We have no plans and no map; we are simply exploring the countryside as we have done many times before in different parts of the world. At the top of a pass (El Alquilar—the Eagle) for no particular reason we take a turn to Pinango, a small mountain village 44 kilometers distant. Initially the paved road is washed out in a few places but otherwise quite passable, but within a few miles it gives way to a gravel road, and then a tortuous, pot-holed, rock-strewn dirt road down precipitous mountainsides. At several places little shrines on hairpin bends mark the spot where drivers have plunged to their deaths in the valleys below; one bend has three such shrines. We stop to check our whereabouts with a curious indian family living in a ramshackle stone farmhouse in high alpine country alongside a ford across a rushing stream—"Pinango: si, si"—and so across the ford and on we go.

I stop a couple of times and try reversing back up the steeper grades to see if the car has enough traction to make it. We know we should turn back but the afternoon is drawing on and we are fearful of getting stuck on the way out. At this altitude it will be cold at night and little babies need to be kept warm. We press on. The "road" drops down the mountainside, switch-backing down a soft-ish, sandy-ish, trail. Privately, I now don't think we can get out without a tow—we have burned our bridges. After many long anxious minutes we come around one more hairpin bend and Pinango materializes below us, nestled in a steep-sided valley. We heave a sigh of relief. We arrive with the village priest right behind us in a four-wheel-drive Toyota jeep. It turns out that he only goes to this remote village once a month. I am eyeing his jeep with a view to a tow and thinking this must be divine providence!

Pinango has no hotels, no restaurants, and nowhere for visitors to stay since no one ever goes there. Terrie takes Paul and goes knocking on doors with her broken Spanish looking for a room to stay. No luck. We are getting a little desperate when the priest offers to put us up in a corn shed attached to the church. We buy three cans of sardines and six small bread rolls from the local store, have an unappetizing meal, and spend a sleepless night huddled together for warmth with no blankets and cardboard for pillows, wearing every stitch of clothing that we have with us.

The following morning we make an early start, expecting to get stuck but knowing that the priest will soon be along. In the end we are all right, although I have to put the family out a couple of times to make hairy slip-sliding runs alongside precipitous ravines. We make it back to the El Aquilar Pass and will not be going to Pinango again. We motor a few miles down the road and come upon the Hotel Los Frailes, a converted sixteenth-century monastery with many of the original buildings still intact. After the night in the corn shed we feel we deserve something first class and so we check in. We have a sumptuous room with a real minstrels' gallery and eat a delicious steak dinner in the old, beamed great hall. It is quite the finest hotel in which we have ever stayed and what a contrast from the night before. The total cost, including dinner, is $22.

In the morning the valley is fogged in. We return to El Alquilar hoping to get above the cloud line but without success. We run back down to Merida and spend more time in that pleasant city. A day or two later we return to Cumana.

We are still waiting on the boatyard. I get down to some serious writing. This is a process that sometimes infuriates Terrie. Once I get immersed, I am dead to the world. As a teenager, when doing my homework I would tune the AM radio to one of the pirate stations then broadcasting rock music illegally into the U.K. and crank up the volume. The sound of Bob Dylan fading in and out would always exasperate my mother; she would ask how I could stand it. My answer—that I couldn't hear it, and that this was my test of whether or not I was concentrating hard enough—did nothing to placate her.

Even in the confined space of the boat there are times when Pippin and Paul are screaming and I am completely unaware! I am getting quite a bit of work done which is bringing me to a realization that there is no way I can meet the deadline on my new book without returning to areas where further research materials will be accessible. I write home: "The new book is already proving quite a task and is going to be hard to complete on schedule (the contract date is the end of October next year). Come the spring I may well have to find a place ashore where I can spread out my papers and really get stuck into it, but where is anybody's guess at present. In the meantime, I continue to get a lot of good ideas and materials from the problems and disasters of people we meet along the way—I am getting to be quite a ghoul going round anchorages asking people about all their gear and equipment failures: the worse the stories, the better I like them!"

The more I work on the book, the less the time Terrie has for her artwork. There is an underlying imbalance here in as much as we are more-or-less financially completely dependent on my writing with Terrie increasingly in a support role. But then Terrie is given an exciting opportunity. A friend, a sailing artist like Terrie, is participating in a two-person show in a prestigious modern art museum on Isla Margarita. The other artist drops out and Terrie is asked to step in.

We hurriedly frame up ten or so of Terrie's watercolors and she flies to Isla Margarita to show them to the museum curator. Paul is breastfeeding and has never been introduced to a bottle—he has to go along for the ride. In the middle of Terrie's presentation his bowels came unglued, flooding his diaper, and dribbling down Terrie's leg onto the curator's spotless white carpet. Oh the trials and tribulations of mothers and artists! Terrie is still accepted for the show but with the date postponed for a year.

A letter home: "Nov. 19. We have had a complete turn-around in our plans. Terrie has been offered a show in a fancy Venezuelan art museum on Isla Margarita, in conjunction with a friend of hers, next August. If we go to Central America we have to work back 1,500 miles against the trade winds—a horrific prospect. So we are going to stay in the islands (probably Antigua and the Virgin Islands) for a few months and then come back here early next summer. Next time I write we should be in Antigua. However, if the wind goes into the northeast (which it sometimes does at this time of the year) I have no intention of fighting it so we may be in Puerto Rico or the Dominican Republic!" Terrie writes to her sister: "Nigel says he's sick of beating into the wind so when we take off he's going to put us on a close reach (we will still be heeled!) and we will see where the wind will take us!"

We meet a very friendly couple, Burke and Lynda Draheim on *NightWatch II*, and spend a fair bit of time with them. When we first started cruising we naively thought that we would meet a number of older couples who would be missing their grandchildren back home and would just love to play with, and perhaps babysit, our children for an hour or two. How wrong we have been! What we have found is that almost all the older couples are on their second marriages, both partners having raised a family and got divorced, and that they are running away from home. Burke and Lynda prove to be an exception, tolerating Pippin and Paul with good humor and grace and regularly treating them to gifts.

Pippin is working especially hard on the terrible twos. She marches up and down the deck practicing with different intonations and hand gestures: "NO, NO, NO." Every time she sees a Venezuelan it is: "NO, NO, NO." We are going through our stock of diapers too fast and so we launch into potty training with limited success and lots of accidents. "Yesterday she was on deck and too quiet—she had pooped and walked in it, up and down the deck, and generally smeared it all over herself and the boat." The decks have to be regularly hosed down, which is how we discover Pippin has intestinal worms. At the same time Paul develops a nasty ear infection so we take them both to the hospital. The service is efficient and free; I try to make a donation but it is turned down. The prescription costs less than a dollar. Many of these poor nations have a basic healthcare service that puts the U.S. to shame.

Finally we make it into the yard. We haul *Nada*, clean the bottom, put on four coats of Montana Red anti-fouling, and are back in the water for $250. The paint is only $15 a gallon and lasts for two years. I don't want to know what is in it. We top up the diesel tank and buy a couple of gallons of kerosene for the stove and oven. Within days we are having trouble with the stove: the Venezuelan kerosene has impurities or a high carbon content that is fouling up our burners. I have to clean the burners with increasing frequency until they will barely hold up long enough to boil the water for a cup of tea. The stove is a constant problem until we can find a fresh supply of kerosene and replacement burners (they are one of the few things I don't have in the onboard stores).

We hang around the marina for Trick-or-Treating at Halloween, with Terrie dressed as an owl and Pippin and Paul as owlets, and to participate in a Thanksgiving bash dockside. Then it is time to cast off our mooring lines and sail up island. Had we known at the time that this was the farthest point we would reach we would not have turned back so readily.

CHECKING OUT OF VENEZUELA turns out to be a bit of a problem when we realize that in our excitement at arriving in Cumana back in June we have seen none of the necessary officials, nor obtained any of the requisite paperwork. The guardia who had come aboard when we arrived were just that—guardia.

We debate simply leaving, but have too many miles of territorial water to clear; should we be stopped we will have major problems. So we devise a cunning strategy. The first document we need is from customs. We enter the office with Pippin and Paul just minutes before the lunch break when we assume the officials will be in a hurry to close up shop. We intend to surreptitiously pinch the children and set them bawling the moment we are asked to show our entry papers so the customs officers will want to get rid of us as quickly as possible. We needn't have worried: in true Hispanic style the officer plays with the children and then perfunctorily gives us the necessary paperwork without checking anything. Armed with this first document we sail through the rest of the procedures.

We have the choice of sailing direct from Venezuela to the Virgins, probably on a close reach, or of reversing the downhill run from Grenada, a hard beat against wind and current, after which we can reasonably expect to reach and run through the islands. We decide to do the latter, working our way east along the Venezuelan coastline and beyond almost to the island of Trinidad, taking advantage of any calms and favorable winds in the lee of the mountains and staying out of the current, before heading north.

Early one morning we motor out of the marina with two sleeping babies. While in the U.S. I acquired a new autopilot. I turn it on in order to raise the sails but *Nada* takes off in circles. The new autopilot is operating in reverse to the old one; the more we move off course the more aggressively it swings us the wrong way! Pippin and Paul choose this time to wake and both start crying. Terrie is hanging onto the pair of them while I steer the boat, read the autopilot manual, and try to find a "change over" pin. I get things sorted and hoist the sails.

A gentle easterly blows across the sheltered waters in the lee of the Peninsula de Araya, giving us time to wash, change, and feed the babies, but all too soon we clear the mainland. Right away we are hard on the wind in confused seas with a lot of motion, the port rail under, and the decks awash. Half the books in the starboard bookcase fly across the cabin and narrowly miss Paul in his baby bed on the port berth. Soon we have two very fussy babies and one rather green-looking mother. Now we have to spend much of the time holding a baby each, and I am more pleased than ever before that I have got the autopilot working so well. When I have to attend to boat duties Terrie holds both Pippin and Paul.

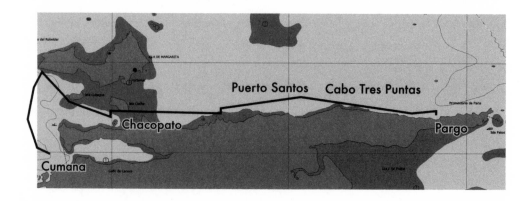

We beat across to Isla Cubagua from Punta Araya looking for some protection but find precious little. From there we press on into the Bahia de Mangle on the southern coast of Isla Margarita. We find calm protected waters—just right for cooking lunch and once again changing the babies who are clearly going to be prime navigational considerations these days. We tack into the lee of Isla Coche past our former anchorage with favorable winds in flat calm seas: 6 to 7 knots close-hauled with not a drop of water over the rail. If only it could be like this all the time. Another choppy little beat puts us back on the Venezuelan mainland in the lee of Punto Morro de Chacopato, a somewhat rock-strewn and poorly charted area rarely visited by cruising yachts. We decide to call it a day and anchor for the night.

The wind fades and the swells ease—a textbook example of the effect of a land mass on the prevailing trade winds. We pull up the anchor and motor due east into a light headwind and substantial leftover swells from the northeast. We are anticipating an offshore breeze and hopefully a flat calm sea as the night wears on but these never materialize. Instead we have a rather uncomfortable night but by daytime are anchored in Puerto Santos having put another precious forty miles of easting behind us. My log notes: "Paul restless with a bit of a wheeze and a dry cough."

After Puerto Santos the coastline becomes increasingly rugged. Three-thousand-foot mountains drop abruptly into the sea; the road comes to an end. The only inhabitants are in one or two isolated fishing villages. The jungle comes to the water's edge; at night there are no lights ashore. We feel more confident that the mountains will give us our much-desired nightly offshore breeze and flat calm seas. In the evening we actually have a west wind in Puerto Santos and eagerly head out but this dies almost immediately. We motor east a half-mile or so offshore in light winds and increasingly calm seas.

The moon sets soon after midnight as we round Cabo Tres Puntas. Here the coastline recedes. In the dark the mountains become indistinct and I have the sense we are moving too far offshore but am reluctant to close the coast in case I am mistaken. A satellite fix confirms that in just one hour we have been swept two miles out to sea by an eddy around the cape. The satnav, when working, is wonderful for this kind of work; radar would be even better, providing a continuous picture of the coastline.

Through the rest of the night we make increasingly sharp course corrections as I consistently underestimate the northward set of the current. I have a problem visualizing how water can keep flowing away from a solid landmass rather than along it! Straying more than a mile or two offshore puts us into the full flood of a branch of the Antilles Current.

Daylight finds us just a mile or two short of Pargo, our destination, the last settlement along this coastline. We are soon anchored. We have completed the last 65 miles of our easting almost painlessly and in spite of two sleepless nights are feeling rather pleased with ourselves.

Pargo is a fishing village fronted by a small beach, surrounded by jungle, accessible only by boat. The one trail out of town peters out quite soon. But even in such an isolated spot news travels fast. We run the dinghy through a moderate surf and up onto the beach. Almost the first question we are asked by one of the fishermen is, "Weren't you in Puerto Santos yesterday?" The local people greet us. Pippin strips off and plays with a crowd of children beneath the village pump—the sole water source. She squeals with delight when a young man hands her a baby monkey and is most upset when she can't bring it back to the boat.

We clamber up the stream cascading through the village, past women washing clothes, and find a little pool in which to bathe. We want to stay but four-month-old Paul's wheeze and cough are a lot worse, and he has thrown up several times in the night. He is now running a fever and clearly deteriorating: we need a doctor, something we will not find in these isolated communities, and are beginning to get alarmed. As evening approaches we pull up our anchors and set course for Grenada, sadly watching the Venezuelan coastline fade into the tropical night.

* * * * *

We are now running really, really scared. Paul is suddenly much worse, coughing and vomiting, struggling for breath, and turning a little blue.

Fortunately, we have a fantastic fast reach all the way to Grenada—the best sail in months—with hardly a drop of water on the decks. Initially, a 15-degree allowance for leeway compensates for the current, confirmed by the satnav which gives us regular fixes. It then goes blank for four hours. The loom of the lights on Grenada coming up over the horizon make it clear the current has strengthened and we are being set to the west.

After 60 hours or so with little sleep, and with *Nada* moving so well, I succumb to lassitude. I sit in the cockpit for the better part of two hours, alternately dozing and thinking I should get up, correct the course, and trim the sails. By the time I shake off my inertia I have to crank in the sheets until we are fairly close-hauled for the final miles up past Salines Point to St. George's. Nevertheless, we are anchored in the lagoon soon after daybreak.

We rush Paul to a doctor who diagnoses asthmatic bronchitis with an infection of the lungs bordering on pneumonia. We are so lucky we had not taken the direct route to the Virgins since it would have taken another day or two longer to reach a doctor and he would without doubt have had to have been hospitalized in serious condition. As it is, the doctor prescribes various medicines and somewhat reluctantly allows us to take him back to the boat. Within twenty-four hours his wheeze begins to clear and he starts to bounce back. What a wonderful relief!

St. George's feels like a familiar friend, though the lagoon is far less crowded since most cruisers have headed north for Christmas. The weather is beautiful—a little cooler than Venezuela with a gentle breeze most of the time. Terrie is enthusiastic about being back. We stay a couple of weeks, giving Paul a chance to fully recuperate. This enables me to work solidly, banging away on my portable typewriter and accumulating piles of typescript while Terrie and the children spend a good bit of time ashore with a young Grenadian family. One way or another, she is managing to paint most days. However, with Christmas fast approaching we decide it is time to continue up island and so say goodbye to our newfound friends. We haul up the anchors.

Our trip to St. Lucia is truly miserable and stands to this day as the most unpleasant passage we have ever made. We are close-hauled the whole way

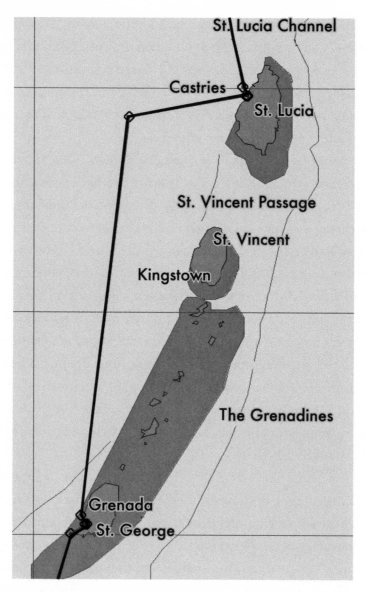

and still set 30 miles by a steady 2-knot westward current. The side deck is continually awash; our open cockpit drenched in spray (we have awnings that we rig when anchored, but no protection at sea). All four of us are soon feeling seasick. Terrie is cradling Pippin and Paul below, the three of them wedged into a berth trying to sleep. Some time in the evening Paul throws up and then Pippin vomits on Paul. The two of them promptly fall back asleep on

Terrie. Terrie, fearful of waking them, tries to sweat it out, which of course is fatal: with the stench of vomit around she soon throws up herself over both of them. Three down, one to go. What a mess. We drag everybody up into the cockpit while I go below to pull out the soiled towels, clothes, and cushion covers, and clean up. That finishes me off. Soon the cockpit is about two feet deep in dirty laundry.

Pippin and Paul are awake. Now they are hungry. I fetch some crackers and bananas and we settle down in the cockpit. Terrie cradles Pippin while I hold Paul. An errant wave strikes the rudder and drives it hard over. The tiller comes sweeping across the cockpit and hits Paul squarely in the head. In the dark we can see a large piece of flesh hanging off his forehead. For a moment both Terrie and I think we have killed him, but then he starts screaming so at least we know he is alive. Panic stricken, we take a closer look: the flesh turns out to be a piece of banana peel that Pippin has thrown away which has been plastered to his forehead by the wind! Paul rapidly settles down but we are badly shaken. Between this scare and his recent illness, together with my recurring back problems, we are ready to hang up the cruising life and settle down. My log reads: "…a terrible fright…in the aftermath of the shock we decided we should quit sailing. We discussed getting the boat tarted up in St. Lucia and then working our way back to the east coast of the USA and selling it."

Later Terrie and the children go below and fall asleep while I continue to beat into the night. The shock has quite unsettled me and sapped my energy. Now I need a crap. I know if I go back inside I will vomit again and probably wake the others, but since we have put the netting around the lifelines I can no longer hang my backside overboard. What a quandary; living in a house is so much simpler than living on a boat! I use a bucket but as I go to pitch it overboard the boat lurches and I send a rather nicely formed turd up the side deck, which is awash. My log reads: "Scrabbling around grabbing turds off the deck and throwing them overboard before the next wave swooshes up the side deck and puts them who knows where." Oh the indignity of it; surely this is rock bottom, but unfortunately we are not quite there.

Shortly thereafter the autopilot goes haywire, making completely random course corrections. The autopilot is a tremendous worry: how on earth are we going to handle the boat and babies without its help? I get *Nada* to self-steer throughout the rest of the night under mizzen and staysail, later adding a double-reefed main. As we move into the lee of St. Lucia the seas settle down and Terrie and the children re-emerge. We motor the final miles to Marigot Bay. My log reads: "The closer we got the more Terrie was talking of carrying on!"

We anchor in peaceful, calm, protected, serene Marigot Bay. In the midst of the gold-plated fleet of boats we wash out our vomit-soaked towels,

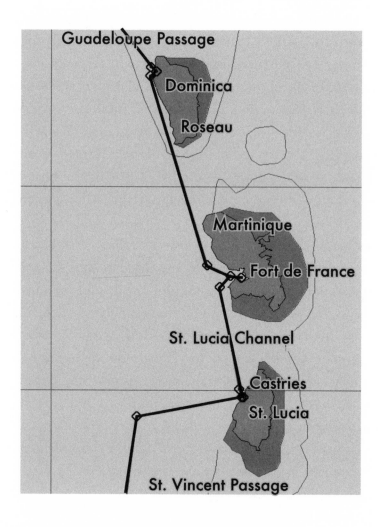

sheets, clothes, and seat covers, and hang them out to dry. We are all asleep by 2000.

The next day dawns clear and beautiful with everyone feeling better. I take the autopilot control unit apart and find a tiny drop of salt water that has penetrated the seals and shorted out a circuit board. I am able to wash it out with a freshwater-soaked Q-tip and put the unit back in commission, which is a tremendous relief. We are physically ready to go on, but mentally something has given.

I tell Terrie that this has primarily been my dream, and it is not working, and that I cannot inflict it on the family any more, and that we should go back to the States and I will find something else to do. Much to my surprise, she is adamant about continuing and giving the cruising life another chance. A little later she sells a number of her watercolors, and so we go back to her favorite haunts to repaint them.

Other matters are also going well: "Found a cure for weevils—two minutes in the microwave!"

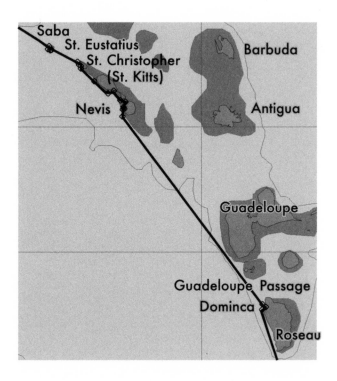

The elements have tested us and we have barely scraped a passing grade, but Poseidon nevertheless takes pity on us. From now on almost the only sail we set is a poled-out jib as we race along at 6 and 7 knots, broad-reaching and running in relative comfort, with breaks on Martinique, Dominica (where we spent a very quiet Christmas), and the Isles des Saintes. With the wind and current on the quarter the world takes on a different complexion. We give Guadeloupe a miss, being fearful of meeting the same obnoxious customs official in Deshaies, and instead run downwind to the little island of Nevis that we passed on our way to Antigua nine months earlier.

CHAPTER 10

NEVIS, ST. KITTS, SINT EUSTATIUS AND SABA
JANUARY 1988

THE HISTORIES OF NEVIS, St. Kitts, Sint Eustatius, and Saba are inextricably linked. The islands all lie within sight of one another and were continually fought over by the British, French, and Dutch. Sint Eustatius (Statia) changed hands twenty-two times! The most turbulent era was during the American War of Independence. The British owned Nevis and uneasily shared St. Kitts with the French. The Dutch controlled Statia and Saba. Nevis and St. Kitts had been extensively developed as sugar producing islands and an enormously wealthy plantation aristocracy emerged on the backs of imported African slave labor (the same was true of the French-owned Guadeloupe and Martinique farther to the south). The colonial policies of the imperial powers dictated that all trade be conducted via the mother country where various customs duties were levied. These decrees, however, were widely circumvented and a substantial, and lucrative, illegal trade developed between the various islands and the American colonies.

Oranjestad, the capital of Statia, was the hub of this trade. The islanders declared the town to be a free port. Here North Americans shipped lumber, tobacco, and corn, and in return bought sugar, rum, and slaves. Furniture and manufactured goods arrived from Europe, and slaves from Africa; sugar and rum were shipped back on the return voyage. The ships that came from Holland were loaded with Dutch-style small yellow bricks and red tiles as ballast that were off-loaded and used by the burghers of Oranjestad to build warehouses and substantial homes. The island merchants and sugar growers grew fat at the expense of European treasuries.

In order to cover their tracks the plantation owners of St. Kitts smuggled their sugar into Statia where it was then shown as a native crop. According to the books this small, somewhat barren, island produced many times as much sugar as the lush, rich, St. Kitts. It was trade issues such as these that were at the heart of the dispute between the American colonists and the British government, finally erupting into war in 1776. Now gunpowder and weapons were added to the stream of supplies reaching the struggling revolutionists, much of this trade financed by the French who were delighted to see their old enemy, the British, embarrassed in this fashion.

Oranjestad became the major trans-shipment point and principal slave market in the whole of the Caribbean. At times as many as 200 ships were anchored off the town waiting to load or unload cargoes. Vast fortunes were made; the island was popularly known as "The Golden Rock." Outraged politicians in London demanded that this trade cease; the Dutch government, unwilling to enter into a conflict with Britain, ordered its colonists to cool it. Instead Statia added insult to injury by firing the first official salute to the new American flag that was flown by the privateer *Andrew Doria* as it sailed into port.

In 1780 England declared war on Holland, and Admiral Rodney took Oranjestad the following year without a fight. His forces hid out for a month, continuing to fly the Dutch flag over Fort Oranje, seizing every ship that came into harbor. He then auctioned off or burned all the spoils of war, the greatest single auction in a hundred years. The merchants and plantation owners of St. Kitts, who suffered enormous losses, never forgave him; he was dogged by lawsuits for the rest of his life.

The French under de Grasse, fresh from aiding the colonists in their famous victory at Yorktown, now turned on St. Kitts. The British defending force of one thousand faced an advancing army of six thousand, but the British had an ace in the hole—Brimstone Hill—an extremely steep 750-foot high volcanic plug—moderately well fortified—that rises up out of St. Kitts' coastal plain. The British landed a number of cannons and a supply of ammunition at the foot of the hill and asked the plantation owners for slave labor to haul this to the top. The plantation owners, still seething at the loss of their goods on Statia, refused to supply the necessary help and the advancing French captured the cannons, turning them on the British. After a month the defending garrison surrendered and the French went on to capture one British island after another until de Grasse and his fleet were finally defeated and captured by Rodney in the Battle of the Saintes later the same year. The French were temporarily driven out of their Caribbean Islands.

* * * * *

We come first to Nevis, almost circular and just six miles in diameter. Approaching from the south, the tip of Nevis Peak comes over the horizon many miles out and slowly the almost perfectly symmetrical 3,000-foot volcanic cone climbs into the sky, its lower slopes curving gracefully into the ocean clad in a sea of coconut palms. We anchor first at Charlestown, an open roadstead guarded by the ruins of Fort George with overgrown cannons scattered around on the ground. Later this anchorage becomes uncomfortably rolly and we move around to a more sheltered spot in Cades Bay.

As we dinghy in to the town dock at Charlestown a local island trader is preparing to depart. The wooden sailing boat is already loaded to the gunwales with boxes when the crowd on the dock drags up half a dozen grown pigs and throws them, legs bound and kicking and squealing, onto the small foredeck. The boat takes off toward St. Kitts, hoisting an enormous gaff-rigged cotton sail.

Nevis is quiet and the people friendly with none of the hustle and bustle we find in most of the other islands—a delightful place to stay. Charlestown is a neat old town with many fine stone and West Indian buildings. Just to the south of Charlestown is a pretty beach backed by a small swamp with coconut trees, sugar cane, and masses of egrets. It is quite a sight to see a palm tree loaded down with dozens of these snowy white birds. To the north of town is the three mile white sand sweep of Pinneys Beach, lined with huge coconut plantations set around still lagoons—considered by many to be the most beautiful beach in the Caribbean (but subsequently home to a large resort).

We rent a car and tour the island, tropical plants and gorgeous flowers everywhere, and monkeys in the trees. Nevis once supported eighty plantations, many with elegant homes, and with over thirty stone windmills facing into the steady trade wind breezes. These mills were used to grind the fresh-cut sugarcane as the first step in extracting its liquid gold. Most of the homes and windmills are in ruins, although a handful have been converted to fine private homes and hotels. The countryside is dotted with boarded-up stone churches, most dating from the seventeenth and eighteenth centuries, mute testimony to wealthy times in the past.

We meet celebrated local artist Eva Wilkins and her brother-in-law Maynard, a one-time manager of sugarcane and sea island cotton plantations on Montserrat, Nevis, and St. Kitts, but now retired. He has built an intricate working model of an old sugar mill and spends time reminiscing on his many years in this often-turbulent business, remembering in particular a devastating strike. The union was out to secure day labor rates in place of the existing piecework; the companies determined to maintain the status quo. After thirteen weeks many of the cane cutters' families were near starvation and the sugar plantations were facing ruin. A "compromise" was reached in which the cane cutters received payment by the day but had to cut three tons of cane a day to get paid—the union saved face while management effectively retained the piece rate.

On the far northern side of the island is the sleepy little fishing town of Newcastle, native boats drawn up on a sandy beach under shady coconut palms with the mountains of St. Kitts across The Narrows in the background. The local children show off to Pippin and Paul, shinnying up the trees to pick coconuts.

In Gingerland, a small village outside Charlestown, we come upon a group of Masqueraders—dancers dressed in colorful robes and peacock feather headdresses who go from door to door collecting money for their performances. The leader of the all-black troupe is also called Nigel. He explains that while the dances look traditionally African, in fact Masquerading is of quite recent origins.

It is December 30th and everyone is beginning to gear up for New Year's, the major Carnival day in these islands. Exuberant St. Kitts is reputed to have by far the more exciting parade so we return to the dock and our boat and the following morning sail over to Basseterre to join in. In the afternoon the children have their own parade with hundreds of fabulous costumes. Halfway through a front passes over and rains out the proceedings. The winds keep up all night while the local steel band maintains a steady beat until 0700 so there is little sleep. New Year's Day dawns clear and bright with excited groups of people gathering all over town. The parade is scheduled to kick off at 1230. It finally gets underway at 1530 but no one is in the least bit bothered.

This is a marvelous carnival: a true all-island and family affair. It is relaxed and friendly with a wonderful community spirit. All the schools have prepared for weeks, resulting in some exotically imaginative costumes. Half of Basseterre is in the parade—the other half chasing it around town. We follow for a couple of hours until my back and the children give out and then retreat to the boat to rest. Later we do a little touring around the island.

St. Kitts is one of the larger West Indian islands, rising to the majestic 4,000-foot volcanic peak of Mount Misery, renamed Liamuiga after independence, which is the old Carib indian name for the island and means "fertile land." The lower slopes of the mountain rise in a gentle arc providing acres of rich, well-watered, arable land. In spite of the vicissitudes of the international market, sugar is still king, with the whole island seemingly covered with the bright green cane. Scattered around the countryside are many gingerbread-decorated West Indian homes.

We catch the bus to Brimstone Hill and drag the children to the top of this sun-baked volcanic outcrop, past immense walls and tier upon tier of gun emplacements, most built by the British following recovery of St. Kitts after their defeat at the hands of de Grasse in 1781, and now fully restored. The entire hill is covered in fortifications, which have earned it the nickname of "The Gibraltar of the West Indies". From the topmost battlements there is a clear view past Statia to Saba in the north, and down to Nevis in the south.

* * * * *

Oranjestad on Statia is just a short sail from Basseterre in the shadow of the cannons on Brimstone Hill the whole way. The anchorage is another open roadstead, untenable in certain conditions. The front that rained out the children's parade in Basseterre has also brought strong south winds to Statia and stripped much of the sand off the beach at Oranjestad, something that apparently occurs regularly. Later wind shifts put the sand back. We are told a hair-raising tale of a 44-foot ketch anchored in 30 feet of water during one of these southerly gales. Its anchors held but the sand that was stripped off the beach built up under its keel until it was smashing the bottom and its hull was stove-in. The conditions are rolly when we arrive but not so bad that we can't live with it.

There is nothing in the way of a natural harbor at Oranjestad that could justify the booming free port of former years. This was purely the product of Statia's central location within the West Indies and the irrationality of international politics. The poor sailors forced to anchor off of this town waiting to load or off-load cargoes must have paid a heavy price in discomfort.

The beach is lined with brick ruins, many of them now underwater—the warehouses, stores, and brothels of the glory years. A winding cobbled road ascends the steep cliffs immediately behind the beach. This is the "slaves' walk" up which the poor, manacled victims of that infamous trade had to stumble to be auctioned off. At the top is Fort Oranje, built in 1636 and fully restored, which was surrendered many times as the island changed hands and never once put up a decent fight.

The upper town was formerly the province of the well-to-do merchants and gentry. Many good-looking buildings, built of the imported small yellow bricks, still remain. Tropical flowers are everywhere. The neat, orderly Dutch presence is immediately felt from the complete lack of hustling to the universally friendly reception we receive. The Dutch islands are the only islands in the West Indies that we find to be clean. A passing motorist stops to chat and then insists on taking us for a tour of the island the next day. This in spite of the fact, as we later find out, that his house burned down just two weeks previously and so he has more important things to do.

Statia has its share of ruined forts and overgrown cannons, looking across the straits to Brimstone Hill in the south, and also to windward on the northeast coast, the likely approach of invaders under sail. We wind around the base of the Quill, a 2,000-foot extinct volcano with an almost perfect rim surrounding a deep crater, at the bottom of which is reputed to be a magnificent tropical rainforest. After some debate we balk at the thought of hauling Pippin and Paul down and content ourselves with seeing the rest of the island.

Our tour guide is a specialist in local herbs and plants. On hearing of my back problems he sends us home with some soursop to brew into a tea and take as a nighttime soporific. I try it that evening. The plant is evidently quite potent. I can feel a benign sense of relaxation creeping up my legs as it takes hold. This reminds me of the story of the Greek philosopher, Socrates. He was executed with a dose of hemlock, which slowly paralyzes the body from the feet up until it reaches, and stops, the heart. While my body grows more and more tranquilized my mind is racing—it is the early hours of the morning before I am able to doze off.

The weather moderates and the swells ease. We decide to head for Saba, which is a notoriously difficult island for yachts to visit. Once again there are no natural anchorages. A small protective harbor wall has been built on the southwest coast at Fort Bay; we make for this. The swells are running heavily from the east with a stiff trade-wind breeze when we arrive. The local fishing fleet is anchored inside the wall and it is necessary to hook around and come up between the fleet and the wall. During the final approach we are more or less broadside to the swells, rolling heavily, the propeller biting air from time to time, our long-keeled boat slow to respond to the rudder and hard to maneuver. As we work around the end of the dock the bow slips into still air while the wind on the stern and a back eddy kick us around as if in a whirlpool. The bowsprit comes flying toward the dock and we narrowly miss smashing it as I go hard astern and beat a hasty retreat. Somewhat shaken we debate giving Saba a miss but I am loathe to give up quite so easily.

We steel ourselves for a second shot and this time are successful, but even well in toward the head of the dock still find a strong surge hooking around behind the wall. With considerable effort we set a breast anchor to hold us off the wall, place all our fenders over the side, and double up on the mooring and spring lines, tying in lengths of chain in place of the lines wherever they lead across the dock and may chafe. This takes quite some time. We are finally preparing to go ashore when a rogue swell throws us against the wall, bursts a fender, smashes our heavy rubrail, and pops a half inch Dacron mooring line as if it is a piece of string. In something of a frenzy we take in the rest of the lines, retrieve our anchor, and bid Saba a sad farewell. We can see how it gets its reputation—it is well deserved.

We sail around the western side of Saba into increasingly protected water. At the northwest tip in Well's Bay we find it is calm, though windy. The wind, hooking around the island, is running straight onto a narrow, rocky beach, backed by sheer cliffs, and with many huge off-lying boulders, making this something of a dangerous anchorage. We find a patch of sand in 20 feet of water in the center of the bay and set two anchors hard. I am confident they will hold in the existing conditions, enabling us to explore ashore.

A road cuts down through the cliffs and dead ends on the rocks. We take the dinghy and potter backward and forward behind the surf line looking for a place to land. The island is tantalizingly close, but with two babies on board and all those rocks ashore plus the boulders in the water, and with a moderate surf running, creating a strong undertow as the breaking waves slide back off the beach, we can see no safe way in. And even if we do succeed in landing without swamping and wrecking the dinghy, what if the seas kick up while we are touring the island? How will we get back to *Nada*?

We turn and motor the two miles around the rocky coastline to Fort Bay, our 2 hp Seagull outboard chugging steadily all the way. This, too, is not without its anxieties. We are in a tiny boat with two babies in the open ocean out of sight of any potential rescuers if we run into trouble and without any form of communication (we have no handheld VHF radio). Our outboard motor is an antiquated piece of equipment. If it conks out, we will have to row; if there is any current, it will be a stiff row.

The Seagulls have been nicknamed "wife beaters" in the cruising community. This is because they are cranked by slipping a knot in the end of a piece of cord into a slot on the flywheel on the top of the motor, winding the cord around the flywheel, and pulling hard. When the end of the cord is reached, the knot comes free and the cord flies off, with the end whipping past whoever is pulling it and hitting anyone behind them! Since it is generally the male in a husband and wife team who does the cranking, it is the wife who gets hit. These are temperamental motors, but once started generally run reliably. Unfortunately, Terrie has always had trouble starting it.

At one point Terrie writes to her sister: "Nigel may have to fly back to the States for a few days. I am in the peculiar position that I can't even get off the boat with two babies! Pippin is fine—she has a life jacket and sits by herself, but I can't use this funny motor on our dinghy and so I have to row which I don't mind most of the time because it's good exercise—but I need to hold Paul and that doesn't work rowing!" We have dreams of something more modern and easier to crank than the Seagull but don't feel we can afford it.

Saba is one sheer cliff after another, most of them too steep even for the wild mountain goats we see balanced on precarious ledges high above us with tropicbirds soaring overhead. We pass through Ladder Bay and there, hewn out of the solid rock, are over 500 steps going straight up the cliff face to a small abandoned customs post. Until quite recently many of the goods brought onto the island have been landed through the surf at Ladder Bay, carried up these steps by hand, and then loaded onto mules and packed to their final destination. From the top of the cliffs the land rises steeply to Mount

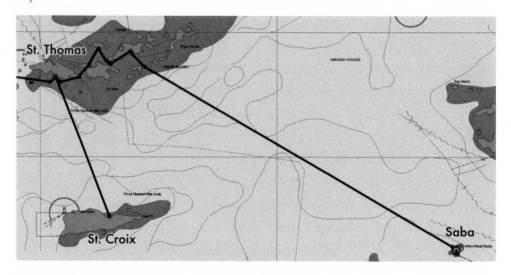

Scenery, a near 3,000-foot volcanic cone. Nothing is flat. We wonder why anyone in his or her right mind would want to colonize this island.

We hug the shoreline to keep out of the worst of the swells as we come around to the south of the island and once again creep into the shelter of the dock at Fort Bay. Here we haul the dinghy onto about three square feet of sand at the foot of the harbor wall and tie off to a streetlight. We check in and begin the arduous trek up the steep road from Fort Bay to the small town of Bottom 800 feet above us, carrying Pippin and Paul and 20 lbs. of camera gear on our backs. Quite soon we are offered a ride, which we gratefully accept and in this fashion are able to see most of the island. We return to *Nada* for the night.

On our second day we dinghy back to Fort Bay and find a ride from Bottom up a twisting, hand-built road to Windwardside, 1,100 feet higher. From there we struggle up the 1,100 steps carved out of the rock that lead to the summit of Mount Scenery. The trail ascends through a tropical rainforest with enormous ferns and vines clinging to the trees and startlingly green vegetation set against an azure sky. Every once in a while we have a clear view to St. Martin, Statia, or St. Kitts with not a cloud in sight.

We march ourselves up, loaded with the children and camera gear. The first couple of hundred steps are not too bad; the next couple of hundred a strain; and from there it gets worse. We are used to backpacking in the Rockies, but even so that last 100 feet is done on willpower, aching in every muscle. As we stagger up the final stretch clouds close in and we climb into a thick fog. After all that effort I take not a single photograph. It takes every ounce of remaining energy to drag ourselves and the children back down, and we are sore for days afterward.

Back on *Nada*, in the evening the wind begins to kick up, gusting strongly toward the rocks, making our Well's Bay anchorage a dangerous lee shore. I spend a sleepless night, repeatedly checking the anchor rodes. The snorkeling is said to be fabulous around Torrens Point, just off our port quarter—we have planned on spending the next day exploring the underwater world—but by the morning the wind is gusting around the point ferociously and it is clear all snorkeling is out. The dinghy ride to Fort Bay with the children will be too dangerous, and there is no way we can make it ashore. I would not, in any case, want to leave *Nada* unattended; Well's Bay is rapidly becoming untenable.

Two days is nowhere near enough to enjoy Saba: the entire coastline out to 200 fathoms is an underwater national park with reputedly some of the finest diving and snorkeling in the Caribbean, and we haven't even put our heads underwater. But Mother Nature is giving us our marching orders, and at least we have been luckier than many a sailor before us who has sailed tantalizingly by without being able to set foot ashore at all. We haul up the anchors, work our way out of the confused wind around the point, pole out a single jib, and tear off downwind toward St. Thomas, arriving in mid-January, 1988.

WE ARE NOT OVEREXCITED at being back in Charlotte Amalie. Within twenty-four hours Pippin, who has just turned two, has cabin fever. Unable to swim or play on a beach, soon after daybreak she wakes and starts chanting: "No boat; no boat" and "Walk on the beach; walk on the beach." After excursions ashore, when told to get back in the dinghy she stages a sit-down strike on the quayside, refusing to have her life jacket put on, throwing a tantrum. "No jacket; no jacket." Paul at 6 months is learning to pull himself up, and as such needs closer watching than ever, while Terrie notes in a letter home: "My life has changed again. We knew our time was short lived—Pippin has given up napping." Pippin and Paul are teething, which does nothing to improve the situation, and both Terrie and I are suffering from a lack of sleep.

But there are also good reasons to be here. The moment we enter the harbor we come upon our old friends Burke and Lynda. We are able to have our mail forwarded to us for the first time in months, including all our Christmas packages. We can pick up supplies not readily available elsewhere in the West Indies. And I begin to dig out answers to many questions thrown up in the process of working on my new book and to gather fresh research material.

The mail is a long time coming; we spend six weeks in the Virgins, returning to Charlotte Amalie every week or so to check in with the post office. In between we cruise around while I work on the book and we are pleasantly surprised by what we find. For a while we are joined by Terrie's brother Mark and his wife Kristin and have a great time with them.

The explosive growth of the bareboat charter fleets has brought hundreds of new boats to the Virgin Islands, but the limited vacation time of most charterers and their lack of local knowledge lead them to follow the same well-beaten paths. The result: a few dozen overcrowded anchorages while close by are still many quiet, relatively unexploited bays.

We make the short sail from St. Thomas to St. John past Christmas Cove, chock-a-block with boats, and through Current Cut with its strong tides and little whirlpools. Much of St. John is a national park with little development. The western and northern coasts offer one picture-perfect bay after another with rocky headlands wrapped around pristine sandy beaches. Unfortunately many are uncomfortable in typical trade-wind conditions while others, such as Caneel, are grossly overcrowded in a most unseamanlike manner.

We find that in the evening in Virgin Island anchorages there is a tendency for the wind to fade. As the tropical night settles in, fluky winds, sometimes with strong gusts, funnel down the steep hillsides from all directions. Add to this a change in the tide, and boats start to weave all over the place around their anchors. It is not uncommon for two boats lying next to each other to swing around in completely opposite circles and end up stern to stern. Take a crowded anchorage, often with poor holding, and soon boats are fouling one anothers' rodes and bumping into each other. We spend several hours at Caneel fending off a latecomer who arrives at sunset, throws down his hook, and dashes in to dinner at the $400-a-night beach hotel.

And yet just three miles or so along the north coast is Francis Bay, a better all-weather anchorage with good holding in a sandy bottom, no hotel, no tourists, an equally enticing beach, and few boats. On our first visit a flock of pelicans greets us with a tremendous display of acrobatics, plunging into the water all around and coming up with a fish almost every time. We blow around our anchor in circles here for three days without coming close to another boat until finally the anchor chain fouls one of the flukes on the Danforth anchor and pulls it out of the bottom. We are exploring ashore at the time. A breathless girl runs to tell us our boat is almost on the beach. We race back to find *Nada* has narrowly missed another boat, but now the anchor has taken a temporary bite just off the beach. We are able to set the CQR before getting into trouble. I have been using the Danforth with mostly a rope rode because it is easier on my back than the CQR and chain, but after this experience the Danforth is relegated to the status of a lunch hook.

Around the corner from Francis Bay is Waterlemon Cay, our favorite anchorage on St. John, perfectly sheltered off a rocky little islet with a white sand beach. In a letter to her sister, Terrie describes our anchoring routine: "we found a lovely bay and decided to try it out. The procedure is Nigel heads the boat up to where we want to anchor and goes up to the bow to drop the anchor and let out the chain. I steer the helm—I am holding Paul—try to keep Pippin in the cockpit, hold the dinghy line from going in the propeller, and work the throttle and gear levers (that's using arms, feet, hands, mouth!). Nigel yells 'neutral' and Pippin yells to me 'neutral.' Quite a little sailor we have here." We find excellent snorkeling with turtles, giant eagle rays, and peacock flounder amongst the coral heads and tropical fish. Hundreds of starfish are scattered over the sandy bottom and up the surfline onto the beach.

Tortola, chief island of the British Virgins, is a scant two miles away across The Narrows. A short beat takes us into Sopers Hole and the British customs at West End. Checking in here is more relaxed and easier than at Roadtown, the capital of Tortola. Once checked in the British Virgins lie in wait.

Another easy beat takes us to White Bay on Jost Van Dyke, with a protected anchorage tucked behind a fringing reef. We snorkel in turns as usual. Terrie finds a seemingly endless school of bait fish—millions upon millions of little minnows, so thick that visibility in the crystal clear water is reduced to just two feet in all directions. As we swim through, the fish part in front of our facemasks and close in behind again. Looking down we seem to be gazing on a field of wheat gently undulating in a spring breeze.

A sudden flurry. Frightened fish scattering in all directions. A hole opens below. And there, little more than an arm's length away, lurks an evil looking 5-foot tarpon. My heart skips a beat as the great fish turns a cold eye on me and lazily glides away. Just as suddenly the minnows close back in and the tarpon is gone. Both Terrie and I come as close to several more that afternoon with the same shock and racing pulse at each encounter, and a sense of wonder when the fish is gone.

Close by White Bay is Great Harbour, home to Foxy's Bar, owned by Foxy Callwood. This is a famous watering hole patronized at one time or another by various celebrities. Quite by chance we have shown up on the weekend of Foxy's annual "birthday party", an event for which cruising boats converge from near and far. Mick Jagger and Jimmy Buffet are rumored to be coming (they are always rumored to be coming).

At nightfall close to 170 boats are crammed into Great Harbour, anchored one on top of another on short scope. Soon the party is in full swing and almost everyone half cut. Later, when it begins to break up, we hear that a number of people can't find their own boats while others end up sleeping on the wrong boat without realizing it. It takes little imagination to visualize what chaos could be caused by a change in the weather or a shift in the wind. And yet we are anchored around the headland, a mere ten-minute dinghy ride away (with our 2 hp Seagull) in company with just four other boats.

While in White Bay, and chatting to the crew on a neighboring charter boat, we make a valuable discovery. Most of the charterers over-order groceries and have a surplus which they are willing to give away when it is time to return the boat to its base. From then on, Friday evenings result in a bumper crop of miscellaneous, and sometimes quite fancy, delicacies!

At the eastern end of Jost Van Dyke is Sandy Cay, a speck of an island owned by one of the Rockefellers and maintained as a botanical garden, and just to the north Green Cay. Both have attractive beaches. A tiny reef fringes Green Cay and when we are there a swell is running. Pippin and Terrie have made friends with a family they met on the beach on St. John; we have picked them up and taken them with us for the day. We have four adults and five children in the dinghy as we putter up and down the reef looking for a break, trying to gauge the right moment to brave the breakers and make a dash for the beach. A series of larger swells catch us broadside and push us into the surf line. A wave breaks into the dinghy and swamps it. We are swept onto the reef before I can shut down the outboard. The propeller hits a rock at full speed and wrecks the lower end. Wet and bedraggled we stumble ashore. After that we have to row until I can find a replacement lower end.

And so to the northern coast of Tortola with few protected anchorages. Cane Garden Bay is crowded and in any case rolly. But we do find a sheltered spot behind Monkey Point on Guana Island with one other boat for company and excellent snorkeling around the rocky headland. Another short reach between Little Camenoe and Great Camenoe brings us to Trellis Bay on Beef Island, one of the most protected anchorages in the region and our jumping off point for a visit to the Baths on Virgin Gorda.

The Baths are a jumbled pile of huge boulders, many bigger than houses, heaped haphazardly one on top of another, spilling into the sea, forming caves, secluded pools, and small beaches, with excellent snorkeling along the faces of the rocks. A magical place but it pays to get there early. The holding is poor (thin sand over rock and coral) and this is one of the prime charter boat stops. We get a tenuous hold with two anchors and spend a wonderful day swimming, snorkeling, exploring, building sand castles, and just plain lazing on the beach. As the day heats up, rocks and scattered coconut palms provide a measure of shade, and there is always the water to cool off.

This is not a recommended overnight anchorage, although we stay on occasion after carefully swimming down and setting our anchors beneath large boulders. To the north is the Yacht Harbour at Spanish Town with full marina facilities (at a price), and then there are anchorages at the entrance to the Yacht Harbour and outside the reef at Little Dix Bay. Neither anchorage has good holding and both prove rolly. But just another mile up the coast we find a protected spot with a sandy bottom behind the reef in Savanna Bay. The half-mile-long beach is deserted, unscarred by anything but bird and animal prints.

A chain of islands—Ginger, Cooper, Salt, Peter, and Norman—lead southwestward from Virgin Gorda lining the Sir Francis Drake Channel back to St. John. We have a fabulous trade-wind reach, water rushing past the bow, the stern wave curling up beside the cockpit, spray in the air, and the tropical sun blazing out of a blue sky. Several times we are drawn back to one particular uncrowded anchorage—White Bay—on Peter Island. It has yet another pretty beach and, at the northern end of the bay, a few isolated coral heads almost on the beach with as concentrated and colorful a display of living coral and tropical fish as we find anywhere in the Virgins. A steep road leads up from the beach to the 500-foot-high backbone of the island, affording spectacular views of almost all the principal Virgin Islands: Virgin Gorda and all the islands between, Tortola, St. John, and Norman Island.

Norman Island is reputed to be the model for Robert Louis Stevenson's *Treasure Island*. It has an excellent protected anchorage in the Bight but it is crowded. The caves around Treasure Point are the big attraction. The water off the caves is deep all the way in. We pass by the Bight and anchor alongside a large three-masted schooner just off the cliffs and a tiny pebble beach. The snorkeling here is great: time and again we are drawn back into the water. In between we explore the dark and eerie caves, rowing in and out in our dinghy. We stay overnight and in the morning half a dozen tropicbirds, with their magnificent long tail feathers, swoop in and out of the cliff face and around our mast tops. They disappear with the shadows as the sun climbs into yet another blue sky. It is time for us to be going too. We haul in our anchors and set sail for St. Croix, 30 miles to the south, and the last of the major Virgin Islands.

With the wind in the east and southeast, and the Antilles Current pushing westward at 2 knots, St. Croix is a lively beat. We have 12,000 feet of sparkling, ultramarine water beneath the keel, and 6- to 8-foot swells forward of the beam; flying fish break out of the wave faces and glide along the troughs; dolphins play in the bow wave. This is true Caribbean sailing once again such as is not generally found in the relatively protected waters between the other

Virgin Islands. Unfortunately, Terrie's brother Mark is seasick and I destroy my camera when we get slapped by a wave while I am taking pictures of the water surging up the side decks.

While he is with us, Mark does us a great favor: he puts the now repaired Seagull outboard motor on the dinghy, doesn't clamp it on properly, and has it flip off the back of the boat into 60 feet of water. He feels guilty enough to replace it—we get the new outboard we have been hoping for!

St. Croix puts us back in United States territory; the port of entry is Christiansted. The well-marked channel zigzags around a number of reefs under the watchful eye of the cannons in the fort; this is no place for a night entry. We find anchorages with good holding in sheltered water on both sides of Protestant Cay, the small island in the center of the harbor. Entry procedures are relaxed and straightforward.

Up until 1917, the Virgin Islands belonged to Denmark. In that year, they were bought by the United States. Christiansted is a fine old Danish town with many colonial buildings and good shopping. In fact, most of the prestigious stores in Charlotte Amalie have an outpost in Christiansted, but here there are no cruise ships since the harbor is not deep enough to accommodate them. There are none of the hassles of St. Thomas; the whole island has a far more laid-back, relaxed, and friendly feel about it. The Danish fort is in pristine condition. In the island's interior several of the old plantation homes have been tastefully restored, lending substance to images of the luxurious lifestyle of the former plantation aristocracy, whose wealth and ostentation rivaled that of the Kings' and Queens' of Denmark themselves. The grounds of one ruined great house have been sculpted into a botanical garden crammed with gorgeous tropical flowers.

A little to the north of St. Croix lies Buck Island, the whole of which, together with its encircling reef, has been made into a national park. We squeeze our 6-foot draft up inside the reef, just inches beneath our keel, to one of the permanent moorings established by the park authority in an effort to prevent the extensive damage done by anchors to coral in the rest of the Virgin Islands. Here we snorkel the Buck Island Trail, a carefully laid out

path through a reef with all the principal types of coral labeled—a fascinating experience for novice snorkelers, but nothing to rival some of the coral we have seen elsewhere.

It is time to check the mail once again, and so we head back to Charlotte Amalie and this time hit the jackpot—cards and packages from England and the States and from many friends we have made in the islands. Our prejudices against the Virgin Islands have been largely dispelled. There is still much that is unspoiled, and nowhere else in the Caribbean is there so much variety so close together in such perfect sailing conditions.

There is something habit-forming about one or two hour sails in reasonably protected waters between anchorages, as opposed to the daylong or more open ocean passages between many of the other islands in the West Indies. Even Charlotte Amalie has its good side: if you catch it on a day when only one or two cruise ships are in town, it is possible to savor its fine buildings, charming streets, and narrow alleyways climbing the steep hillsides without having to struggle through hordes of people intent on rushing from one store to the next as quickly as possible. Pippin gets a kick out of clambering up the many flights of steps; coming down, however, is another matter.

* * * * *

Boatowner's Mechanical and Electrical Manual is progressing rapidly, but in the process growing by leaps and bounds. For every question that is answered two more emerge that remain unanswered. I am also accumulating a mass of illustrative material; it begins to look as if the finished work will be 400 or 500 pages long with over 600 illustrations, posing a major challenge to the production crew at International Marine. The further I get into this project the clearer it becomes that the publisher and I will not be able to resolve last minute technical problems over Third World phone lines. We do not have the facilities on board, and available to us when cruising, to see this book through to the finish; we need to return to the States for an extended period.

Terrie writes to her sister: "Surprise, surprise! Instead of heading south for Venezuela we've decided to come back to the States for a while. Nigel has much work to do on the final phase of the book and needs to spread out…in any case sailing is nearly impossible with Paul crawling and trying to walk."

For the third time in a little over a year our cruising plans are thrown into confusion. We have a choice of leaving *Nada* in the Caribbean and flying home, or of sailing back and returning whenever we can. It is not an easy choice. With all the work we have put into building our boat we find it hard to countenance the thought of leaving *Nada* for an unspecified period of time in an area subject to hurricanes and where security is not the best. But on the other hand if we sail back we will be casting away 1,500 miles of precious easting, hard won against the prevailing winds and currents. In the end the decisive factor is the uncertainties in our future: if something arises to hold us in the States, having *Nada* in the Virgins will cause a major headache. We decide to sail back.

* * * * *

A short downwind sail from St. Thomas brings us to Culebrita, one of what is known as the Passage Islands, with a particularly attractive anchorage on the northern side of the island. It is one of those rare jewels in the Caribbean—an island that time and the tourist industry have passed by.

We are in our own little universe, the only inhabitants on the island, which is roughly a mile long and half a mile wide with this one protected bay. There is a sandy beach in front of us with sea grapes and the odd coconut lining the shore, and dramatic rocks to the north providing a splendid back drop for *Nada*. We wander the deserted beaches, our footprints and those of a wild pig the only marks in the sand, and wade in solitary pools at the foot of imposing cliffs.

A sandy trail leads from the beach to the windward side of the island across a narrow low-lying isthmus. Here the Atlantic surf thunders on the beach and headlands, throwing clouds of spume high in the air. Here, too, is a mass of plastic garbage pitched overboard in the Virgin Islands and carried inexorably westward by the trade winds and Antilles Current—a sorry indictment of our disposable era.

The trades whistle up the hillside, the stunted bushes hunched over in serried ranks looking for all the world like waves sweeping up to the lighthouse crowning the hill. There is a trail of sorts to the top from this side of the island, once wide enough for a carriage but now alternating open grassy spaces with all but impassable thickets of thorn. The path curves around to the lee of the island away from the ocean breezes. The hillside is steep, the climb hot and airless. It is quite a while before the tip of the lighthouse peeks out above the bushes. Then we break through the last of the undergrowth onto an open grassy summit. In the center is the bleak, boarded up lighthouse, a lonely sentinel over this long-abandoned island.

We survey our little kingdom from this hilltop. To the east we can see St. Thomas where the winter tourist season in the Virgin Islands is in full swing with boat piled upon boat in crowded anchorages; to the south Vieques; to the north Cayo Norte, another uninhabited island with a most inviting coconut-lined beach; and to the west Culebra, with Puerto Rico in the far distance. Below us *Nada* rocks gently at anchor. Terrie writes to her sister: "No boats here and yet just a few hours from hustling, bustling St. Thomas. Sure is fun to have all these pretty places to ourselves. Paul is cutting his first two lower teeth. Lots of nights when he gets me up every two hours— remember all that?!"

An almost continuous reef links Culebrita to Culebra. After almost a week in our idyllic surroundings, a short reach in boisterous Atlantic swells allows us to duck back into sheltered water as we sail over to Culebra. On this island's southeast coast we find another deserted anchorage, tucked in amongst the mangroves that line the inlet behind Isla Pela. A fringing reef ensures smooth water while the trade winds keep the boat cool and any bugs at bay. Along the outer edge of the reef are many conch.

Just around the corner lies Ensenada Honda, a two-mile-long inlet, protected by a reef with a narrow entrance channel, and with excellent holding and adequate depths throughout, reputedly one of the best hurricane holes in the entire Caribbean. Numerous indentations form sheltered anchorages in any weather. Almost everywhere it is possible to cast out a stern anchor and run the bow into the mangroves. If the fringing wall of mangroves is pushed out of the picture, the scenery around the bay is surprisingly reminiscent of some of the drowned river valleys in southern England; not as green, but with gentle hills and a patchwork of pastures and small woods.

Almost all the island from here eastward is part of a wildlife refuge, protecting sooty terns, brown boobies, and red-billed tropicbirds. In early spring the waters and beaches around Culebra are a spawning ground for turtles; naturalists and volunteers congregate to count the annual hatch. Other parts of Culebra have been, until recently, a gunnery range for the U.S. Navy. This has discouraged visiting yachts.

With the navy gone the island has remained relatively undisturbed, protected by its numerous reefs and, surprisingly, its downwind location from the Virgin Islands. The charter fleets have put it off limits for fear of wrecked boats or incompetent sailors unable to make the sometimes hard beat back to St. Thomas. Apart from two annual sportfishing tournaments, when thousands pour over from Puerto Rico for the weekend, almost the only visitors are the occasional cruising sailors working their way to and from the Virgin Islands via Puerto Rico and the Dominican Republic rather than the more popular direct path from the U.S. Atlantic east coast.

At the head of Ensenada Honda lies Dewey, a sleepy little town and the sole settlement on Culebra, straddling a narrow neck of land between an inlet on the west coast and Ensenada Honda itself. The main street runs from shore to shore; a dinghy cut opening into a small lagoon connects the two bodies of water. Customs is a short walk from either side; clearance procedures for those coming from, or going to, the Virgin Islands free and relaxed. The town boasts a couple of grocery stores, restaurants and bars, a hotel by the ferry dock, and a surprisingly well-equipped dive shop. This is about it.

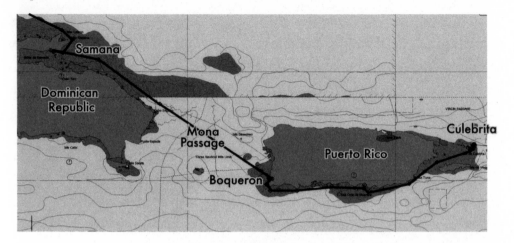

Culebra is Puerto Rican territory and peopled by Hispanics. The contrast in the atmosphere from St. Thomas is immediate and makes a welcome change. The combination of year-round sheltered waters and friendly locals has led a number of people to leave boats here for months at a time, something that is unthinkable almost anywhere else in the West Indies. One or two long-time cruising couples have come and never left, living aboard and running small businesses ashore. They will keep an eye on unattended boats for a small monthly fee.

We leave *Nada* on a mooring for several weeks, flying to England to show off baby Paul to his grandparents and giving me an opportunity to answer a mass of questions thrown up by my new book, and to collect more information. When we return to *Nada* with piles of new manuals, we consider leaving her on the mooring and flying back to the States from Puerto Rico, but in the end decide to sail on. It is just as well.

The following year Hurricane Hugo makes a direct hit on Ensenada Honda and destroys well over a hundred boats that have sought shelter in the bay; only a handful come through unscathed. A number of boats are driven clear up onto the runway for the small airport. Dewey is devastated. Months later, the Army Corp of Engineers brings in a barge and a large crane, picks up the wrecked boats, and dumps them out at sea. Fortunately for us, we have long since sailed on.

Three overnight runs see us back in Puerto Plata in the Dominican Republic after brief stops in Boqueron (Puerto Rico) and Samana, where Terrie shows off Paul to her old friend Chiki. Mangoes are 24 for a dollar, as compared to 12 in Boqueron and 3 in St. Thomas. The children love them, but it's an incredibly messy business. Before eating, they are stripped naked and put into the cockpit where we can hose them and *Nada* down afterward!

ON THE DOCK IN Puerto Plata we are greeted by people who seem familiar—it is the couple whose boat we nearly tangled with when we dragged our anchor in Francis Bay on St. John. Carl and Mary Beth are, like us, headed back to the States, and since we all wish to see the Citadelle in Haiti we arrange to sail together to Cap Haitian.

We have a wild overnight passage. It is downwind so I hank on the genoa before leaving port. However, as we emerge from the shelter of Puerto Plata we find the wind much stronger than expected. Soon we are rushing along under the single poled-out genoa, *Nada* accelerating to 9 knots down the wave faces and close to being completely out of control. It is exhilarating sailing, but the wind and seas continue to build, and we are mildly pooped a couple of times as the crests of waves surging up from astern break into the cockpit. Pippin gets mad and points a finger at the sea. "If you do that again I'll spank you."

Terrie takes the helm while I claw down the genoa and gasket it off to the lifelines. We continue to do 6 knots under bare poles so I don't bother to put up another sail. Toward dawn the wind eases and our boat speed falls off so I reset the genoa. An hour or two later we sail into the calm waters of the bay at Cap Haitian. Two enormous range markers on a high headland guide us in past a ruined French fort; a friendly fisherman gives us a welcoming wave from his little wooden boat. We slip into a berth at the small "marina," which dates from the time of Baby Doc and is more or less abandoned.

And so begins the daily round of petty harassment. First we need a watcher for the boat ($5 a day) to "protect" it. Next the port captain and customs and immigration come aboard. No bribery here but we are asked to change $40 into local currency for the port captain. This becomes a familiar theme. Dollars are a precious commodity, necessary for escape to the U.S., the local currency (gourds) being worthless outside Haiti. It is impossible to go anywhere without a "guide" attaching himself to the party in expectation of a tip; children and adults alike everywhere pester us remorselessly for a dollar.

Hours later Carl and Mary Beth make it in. Theirs is a much smaller boat and they have had a rough, and mildly terrifying, night, with a lot of water breaking over the boat. Whereas we slipped into a finger pier with just our long bowsprit reaching out over the dock, they pull up alongside. This is a mistake: they are immediately assailed by a crowd of young men shouting and fighting over who is to be their watcher. After the hubbub subsides and they are checked in we set about organizing a ride to the Citadelle, the principal reason for all of us to be here.

* * * * *

The Citadelle is the product of a violent and turbulent history and of an ex-slave's megalomania and paranoia. Haiti, once known as Saint-Domingue, was formerly France's, and perhaps the world's, richest colony. A few thousand plantation owners and their families reveled in spectacular luxury while close to half a million slaves sweated and died in the sugar plantations. In 1789 the French, who had so readily aided the American colonists in order to weaken the British, reaped the whirlwind of democratic ideas set in motion by the American War of Independence. The great French Revolution annihilated the old autocracy in France and unleashed a hurricane wind of change in her colonies.

The slaves arose en masse. Thousands of whites were slaughtered; hundreds of plantation homes razed to the ground. The whites retreated to the cities and retaliated with immense brutality: an estimated 10,000 blacks were executed, many of them broken on the wheel, a form of torture popular in medieval times. But then in 1793 revolutionary France decreed the abolition of slavery in Saint-Domingue and regained a tenuous hold on the situation. Several ex-slaves rose to commanding positions in the French army. The most famous, Toussaint L'Ouverture, successfully fought off an invasion by a British expeditionary force.

In 1801 Toussaint L'Ouverture declared independence from France and had himself installed as president for life. Napoleon Bonaparte dispatched seventy ships and an army to crush the rebellion. L'Ouverture was captured and sent to France where he died in jail. The revolt continued under the leadership of another ex-slave, Dessalines. Guerilla warfare and yellow fever drove the French out, with the loss of 50 generals and 45,000 men. On January 1, 1804, Dessalines renamed the new nation "Haiti" after an old Arawak Indian name and had himself proclaimed governor general for life. The same year he ordered the massacre of the remaining whites on the island and assumed the title Emperor of Haiti. Less than two years later he was assassinated by one of his own supporters.

Out of this maelstrom yet another ex-slave, Henri Christophe, born on St. Kitts, emerged as the first president of a new republic. Within a year or two he declared himself King Henri I of all Haiti, but a rival succeeded in splitting the infant nation in two, carving out his own kingdom in the south. Henri Christophe instituted a new and bloody dictatorship. Although he built roads, established schools, and returned the fertile northern plain behind the city of Cap Haitian to rich, productive agriculture, he is primarily remembered for the inauguration of a black nobility, living in great splendor, and the two crowning symbols of his new order: the palace at Sans Souci and the Citadelle overlooking his kingdom, built between 1805 and 1820.

Just as in King Henri's day, when we arrive Cap Haitian is still the principal city of northern Haiti. The Hotel Henri Christophe, from which he peddled influence before seizing power, remains in business. Many of the old colonial buildings are intact, surprisingly sound after years of neglect. There are no pigs running down the main street as we have been led to expect, but cars are few and far between. Sweating laborers haul carts piled high with large wooden barrels from the local distillery; lean-looking donkeys rest in whatever shade they can find.

Before first light each morning dozens of fragile little fishing boats set out to sea from just across the bay. Around noon they come streaming back, their sails a patchwork quilt of scraps of cloth, some in tatters, frequently tied to masts and booms of knobby branches still with the bark attached; an incredible sight, whether silhouetted against the modern ships in the harbor or Haiti's majestic mountains, ever present in the background. Just across from our berths the fishermen have to round a small point of land where half a dozen crude wooden boats are under construction for the perilous trip to Miami. After a day or two in here it is easy to see why so many are willing to risk their lives to escape the island's grinding poverty. One young man who hangs around at the marina claims to have made eleven unsuccessful attempts to flee.

This is the poorest nation in the western world and yet prices are high. Sugar, a local crop, is five times as dear as in the neighboring Dominican Republic, which occupies the eastern half of the same island. Henri's Citadelle is almost within sight of Cap Haitian and yet it costs us, after some haggling, $60 to rent a four-wheel-drive jeep to get there and back. Afterward we realize why—it probably cost that much to fix the suspension!

The road out of Cap Haitian passes through a market district. Smoking charcoal braziers and ramshackle corrugated tin stalls are interspersed with stacks of tree limbs. Now the bare mountainsides around the city are explained—almost all cooking is done on wood or charcoal fires. In a desperate search for fuel the Haitians have been denuding their island of trees, allowing the rains to wash the thin topsoil off the steep mountainsides. In time much of Haiti will be a desert.

After the market we pass the most appalling slums we have seen anywhere, and then cross a bridge into open countryside. Here and there the road is lined with colorful little houses of mud on stick frames (wattle and daub), with thatched or tin roofs and neatly trimmed hedges of prickly pear cactus. In between are unkempt fields of sugarcane and lush green pastures. Now and then we receive friendly waves. Quite soon, ahead of us, the small town of Sans Souci appears, the main street rising steeply to a spacious, white-domed Roman Catholic cathedral and lying next to it the ruins of Henri's palace.

Church is in session, the cathedral packed, the rich tones of hundreds of singing voices drifting melodiously through open doors over the town below. In the cathedral courtyard stand the pillars of the palace gates, leading to the imposing facade of the ruined palace itself, all but destroyed in an earthquake in the 1850s. To the right are the remnants of a second palace, built for Henri's queen. Local legend has it that she only entered his palace when summoned to his bedchamber.

Not even his luxurious lifestyle could drown out Henri's fears of a second invasion by Napoleon Bonaparte. He maintained a large standing army and initiated construction of an impregnable fortress to protect his kingdom—the Citadelle atop a 3,000-foot mountain behind his palace. He ruthlessly poured the resources of his tiny nation into this enormous project, designed to deter the world's greatest power.

Henri is supposed to have ridden daily from the palace to inspect the construction work at the Citadelle. We follow in his steps, our jeep struggling up the tortuous cobbled road hewn out of the mountainside by slave labor (it is one of those ironies of history that after seizing power the ex-slave promptly re-enslaved a goodly portion of his populace). At an area known as the Second Redoubt the road becomes impassable. Teams of Haitians with horses and local artifacts wait to badger any tourist that comes that way. For $2.50 a horse, $1 for the horse handler, and $1 for a horse goader, who whips it periodically from behind, we carry on, now mounted like King Henri himself. Two or three additional children attach themselves to each horse, earnestly explaining in broken English that it is customary to buy them a cold drink at the top and tip them a dollar as well.

I am not comfortable on a horse at the best of times. With Pippin perched on my Pelican camera gear suitcase, which is resting on the pommel of the saddle in front of me, and a crowd of Haitian children running alongside, shouting and prodding the horse, tugging at the reins and whipping the poor emaciated beast into a trot, I am fast becoming a nervous wreck. The mountain falls away steeply to our left; the "road" is a mass of potholes and loose rocks. Every time the horse stumbles I have visions of the saddle slipping and Pippin dashing her brains out. Ahead of us Terrie, born on a horse, appears quite at ease with nine-month-old Paul.

We come around the mountainside and there is the Citadelle high above, drifting in and out of low clouds like some vast medieval castle, an incomprehensible sight in this desperately impoverished nation. The trail steepens and worsens. My nerves get the better of me. Much to the amusement of the crowd, while the horse handler rides the horse, I struggle up on foot, Pippin on my shoulders and the sweat stinging my eyes. I know how that poor beast feels.

The closer we get to the Citadelle the more mind-boggling it becomes. Perched on the top of a mountain this monumental fortress is in excellent shape. The trail leads to the base of its massive, 130-foot high walls, threading around fallen cannons, through a narrow gateway, and up a steep flight of steps. Inside, thousands of cannonballs still stand in neatly stacked piles in the courtyards and gun galleries, ready for use; dozens of cannons on enormous wooden carriages peer out through embrasures, standing sentinel over the fertile plains of northern Haiti below.

Captured bronze cannons weighing over 2 tons apiece were hauled by hand from the coast all the way to the top. They are still here, in perfect condition, bearing the noble crests of Louis XIV of France and George III of England. According to our guide, 20,000 slaves died struggling up this mountainside during the 14 years it took to build the Citadelle. At one point Henri had every tenth slave in line shot "pour encourager les autres" (to encourage the others).

A foundry was established in the Citadelle and hundreds more iron cannons were cast on site. A huge powder room was built which blew Henri's son to kingdom come when he carelessly wandered in with a lighted cigarette. The acres of roof drained into a massive central cistern. Believable or not, the guide informed us Henri quartered 2,000 soldiers here permanently, with enough water and supplies to hold out for years.

The Citadelle is ringed on three sides by mountains. On an adjacent peak is another small, ruined palace, built for the queen in the event of an invasion. To the north, far below, the countryside is flat and fertile, threaded by a narrow ribbon of river, merging into a general haze over the distant Atlantic Ocean.

We turn and make the stumbling ride down to our jeep. A heated argument develops over just how many helpers are entitled to a tip. More and more of the onlookers join the discussion; our driver pulls away, a few stubborn children running alongside, struggling to keep up, shouting after us as we bump and crash down the rutted road back to the palace of Sans Souci.

In 1820 King Henri had an accident that paralyzed him from the waist down. He hid in this palace, suffering from paranoid fits that his enemies would come for him and he would be unable to escape. On October 8, he shot himself through the heart with a silver bullet (some say gold). Henri did not immediately die. His queen assembled a party of bearers to haul the mortally wounded monarch up to the Citadelle. On the mountainside the bearers abandoned him and ran away, leaving the king to die. The queen assembled another party and finally brought the body to the top where it was unceremoniously dumped into a pile of freshly mixed mortar. The cement pile, with the body inside and a little plaque on top, is there to this day.

Back in Cap Haitian we discuss politics with our boat watchers. Since the ouster of Baby Doc the high hopes of the people have not been realized. Inflation is rampant, and the few cruise ships that used to come to Cap Haitian no longer call there, dealing a savage blow to the local economy. Political instability, the constant hassles, and the association of Haiti with AIDS in the public mind have turned the ships away, although from time to time one still anchors out in Labadie Bay on the north coast. Here cruise organizers can control the street vendors while their passengers luxuriate on a classic palm-fringed Caribbean beach, safely insulated from the reality of life in Haiti.

Our last day in Haiti is a Sunday. All day long a small crowd of onlookers, dressed in their Sunday best, stand on the dock taking in Carl and Mary Beth's, and our, daily routines. Mealtimes cause a special stir. Every move in the galley is greeted with a subdued murmur, a mass of faces straining to see through portholes and peer around hatches. Pippin coming on deck in her customary nakedness raises a cheer! When the tropical night closes in the Haitians abruptly melt away.

We have hopes of an early departure Monday morning, but these are dashed by bureaucratic officialdom—impersonal and inefficient, but without malice. And then a flurry of requests for tips, a final settlement with our watcher, not happy at receiving partial payment in gourds, and the dock lines are cast off. It has been an exhausting visit. The Citadelle is one of those places that has to be seen to be believed—we are certainly not sorry we have come and would stop again given the chance—but the dismal slums and the constant wearying pressure to extract a dollar from any tourist depress the soul.

We have been to many poor islands, but none where the unending poverty has so eaten into people's self-respect and so undermined human dignity. There has been little hostility and we never felt any sense of danger, but then there is also no sense of hope for the future. Two days after we leave Colonel Namphi appears on television waving an Uzi sub-machine gun to announce yet another despotic military dictatorship, just another step in Haiti's seemingly unstoppable slide into self-destruction. In 2010 a massive earthquake deals another body blow to these poor people, followed, in 2016, by one of the most powerful hurricanes ever recorded.

* * * * *

We have a fast and lively passage to Great Inagua where we rest a day or two and take in the flamingoes before sailing the 500 miles or so direct to Key West through the Old Bahama Channel. This too should have been a fast voyage with the wind and current behind us. Instead we pass through a succession of calms and light headwinds with a 1-knot current against us. At least no one is bothered by seasickness although at one point Pippin calls out: "Mummy, I feel sick." Her throat and stomach are moving in little spasms. Oh no, we think, how can this be in such easy conditions. "Mommy," she says, "I'm farting in my throat." She has the hiccups.

On the afternoon of the second day while virtually dead in the water we find ourselves on a collision course with a container ship. It brings back memories of the 1971 collision in the North Sea. On that occasion we were becalmed, our motor was out of commission, and we could not get out of the way. On this occasion, too, the ship fails to respond to the radio and continues coming straight at us in broad daylight. We crank the motor and power out of the way. I am sorely tempted to shoot a flare onto the bridge as the huge vessel rushes by.

We cut across the Bahama Channel and find a favorable countercurrent outside the Cuban 3-mile territorial limit. For 36 hours we hug the Cuban coastline, keeping just over 3 miles off. As we round the northern coast on our fourth night out we continue to stay close inshore in order to keep out of the Gulf Stream which flows through the Straits of Florida in the opposite direction at 3 knots or more. Terrie is on watch.

All of a sudden all hell breaks loose. A powerful spotlight holds us completely dazzled while engines roar and a boat comes tearing alongside. Is it

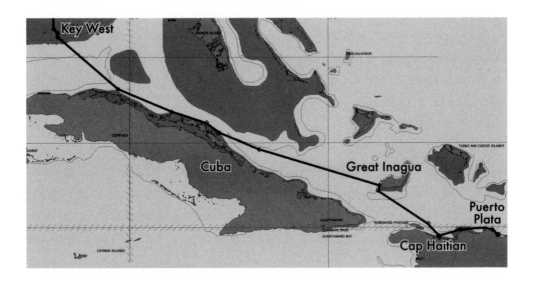

drug smugglers? Our hearts pound; our pulses race. And then we can pick out a large cannon on the foredeck illuminated in the sidewash of the spotlight—a Cuban gunboat. We have no time to feel relieved. They are coming so close I think they will run into our downwind pole. We are being yelled at in Spanish through a megaphone but we can't make out anything above the noise of the engines as the skipper keeps shooting up alongside and then falling back a few yards. We crank our motor and I run forward to drop the downwind pole before they smash it. After that we concentrate on trying to make out what is being said.

It is all academic in any case since there is no way they will be able to hear any answers we may shout to their questions. We are resigned to being towed into Havana when they begin to shout: "Al norte; fuera, fuera. Al norte; fuera, fuera." (Go north; get out, get out.) We put the helm hard over and motor north. They follow for a while and then abruptly wind up their engines and tear off into the night. We reset some sail and try to relax. The rest of the trip into Key West is a welcome anti-climax.

We check in with the customs at Key West, excited to be back in the States and almost home although Terrie writes to her sister "there's a sadness for me with the realization of the possible end of our sailing adventures for a while, but I do love Key West—lots of hippies about!" We are visited by a couple that is thinking of buying a boat and want to know what the cruising life is like. We show them over the boat. Paul, who is sleeping naked in the cockpit, wakes, pulls himself up, and pees through an open porthole over the galley dishrack and all over the galley. It does not seem to dampen our visitors' cruising ardor.

We are once again engaged in potty training. "Dear Mum and Dad… Paul has to do everything Pippin does, including sitting on the toilet. To start with we could get away with leaving his nappy on, but now he gets quite agitated, says 'pee pee' and the nappy must come off. He strains for a moment, nothing comes out, and he gets off feeling very pleased with himself. The nappy then goes back on. The other day he actually did a 'poo poo.' I don't know who was more surprised—him or Terrie!"

Just the Gulf of Mexico to go. This time we decide to make it easy on ourselves and to cover it in stages. To make things even easier, on the first leg to Boca Grande we set out in mid-afternoon so that the majority of the trip will be done at night with the children asleep. As we leave Key West we pass alongside a coast guard cutter. Toward evening this same cutter comes powering out of the Key West Channel, takes a turn around us to check us out, and heads back in. Later that night we have another vessel apparently on a collision course. We hail them on channel 16 and raise the U.S. Treasury cutter *Dagger*. They come close by and keep us company for some time, interrogating us extensively before finally wishing us "Bon Voyage" and leaving. There certainly is a lot of activity in these waters!

The wind is not being cooperative. At Boca Grande we cut into the Intracoastal Waterway but after running aground in its shallow waters decide we would rather take our chances in the open ocean. All the junk acquired in our travels is weighing us down. Another couple of days of frustrating sailing, during which Pippin complains of a stomachache and announces that "a beach would help it," brings us to a protected anchorage behind Punta San Blas in

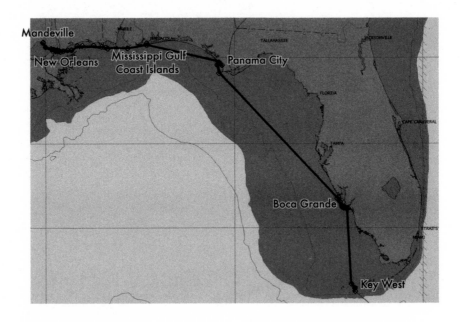

the Florida panhandle with mussels, clams, and softshell crabs in the grassy flats.

Following a stop in Panama City with two more groundings and a sail along the Alabama coastline we are into the Mississippi Gulf Coast Islands. A few more hours and we enter the Rigolets. We are getting really keyed up now, and finally we have the wind and tide astern as we make our way into Lake Ponchartrain. We positively tear across the lake in perfect sailing conditions as the sun sets. Later that evening we pick out the light at the entrance to Mandeville Harbor. This is one harbor we do know how to enter after dark: we drop the sails and motor slowly into and up Bayou Castine. We find our old slip empty, although we have told no one we are coming, and ease right in. We are home.

POSTSCRIPT (2018)

WE MOVED ASHORE for 18 months—long enough to get Pippin and Paul out of diapers and potty trained. For a while we stayed in Montana, living in the basement of Terrie's sister's house. I hired a young Mormon lady, one of 14 children born to a mother who was one of 17 children, to re-type my *Boatowner's Mechanical and Electrical Manual*. It was now approaching completion and consisted of over a thousand pages of cut-and-pasted typescript. The book was published and became an almost immediate success.

This was to be the last book I produced on a typewriter. Soon after, I acquired a Mac. It had a 256k memory and cost $1,500. For another $1,000 I bought a 1mb external hard drive that was almost as big as the Mac. I wrote the first draft of this book on it. The Mac was so slow I had to break the chapters up into individual files so that when I saved a file it did not take forever. When everything was written, I merged all the files into a single file. On reading through the manuscript I found a double space between two words, removed it, and pressed the "save" button. While this was in process, we had a power cut. I lost the entire book, which I had not backed up anywhere else! Panic-stricken, I drove the Mac and hard drive to a computer whiz in Billings, Montana, who managed to recover the file, but only as a continuous stream of words with no punctuation. It took me a while to sort that out and I have been somewhat more diligent about backing up ever since!

I poured everything I then knew about boats and boat systems into the *Boatowner's Mechanical and Electrical Manual*. I imagined I had nothing more to write on this subject and, with two small children, would need another way to make a living. I began work on a series of historical novels. Terrie and I bid on a small farm in the Clark's Fork Valley, Montana, at the foot of the Beartooth Mountains where we have spent so many summers hiking and fishing, and, when the bid failed, considered buying a motel. Luckily none of this came to fruition because the *Boatowner's Mechanical and Electrical Manual* began to put me on the marine map; I had magazines asking for articles instead of rejecting my freelance submissions. It was looking as if, between the books and magazines, I could make enough of a living to maintain us in our low-budget lifestyle.

We took stock of our situation and brought our cruising plans into line with our limitations. Like so many before us, we had set out with romantic dreams about cruising; these had been battered but still lived on. I recognized that we would never be world-girdling sailors, but so what? Right on our back doorstep in Louisiana we had the whole of the Caribbean side of Central America to explore, and we had yet to reach the San Blas Islands.

We went to work on *Nada* to make her leaner and fitter. We installed a roller reefing headsail and electric anchor windlass to take much of the load off my back. The children by now were older, more independent, and above all more stable: Pippin at least could retain her footing, and move around unaided, at sea. In December 1989 I recruited a friend to act as crew. He and I sailed *Nada* across the Gulf of Mexico to Isla Mujeres on the Yucatan peninsula, where he left. Terrie and the children caught a cheap flight into neighboring Cancun to re-join *Nada*.

We went on to explore the northwest Caribbean—the Yucatan, Belize, Guatemala, and the Bay Islands of Honduras—with its numerous protected and rarely visited anchorages and relatively short passages in between. The charts were almost entirely based on surveys conducted by the British Navy in the 1830s and 1840s, copies of which I was able to obtain from the British Admiralty archives. Some areas had never been charted.

Using the dinghy in shallow areas with a pole marked off in feet, and a hand bearing compass to establish crossed bearings, we corrected the charts and created numerous additional anchorage charts. We ran *Nada* aground dozens of times (on one memorable occasion, when exploring Turneffe Reef, four times in one day). The children learned the minute we hit the bottom to go below and keep quiet; Terrie and I learned how to launch the dinghy, row out a kedge anchor, and haul ourselves off without talking to each other.

We sailed back to Louisiana for hurricane season, returning to the northwest Caribbean on four more occasions. We produced a cruising guide to this region, and then, in 1995, circumnavigated Cuba and produced a cruising guide to Cuba.

We were the first boat since the Cuban revolution to be given a permit to explore almost the entire Cuban coastline (one or two areas were off limits). It took a bit of doing to obtain the permit, including a long, stressful nine days under arrest, suspected of being CIA spies, with a large gunboat behind us and armed guards posted dockside to keep watch. But then the Cubans decided a guide would help to boost their tourist industries. Thereafter we were able to enter almost every navigable bay and river on the coast of Cuba, creating around 200 anchorage charts.

Prior to sailing to Cuba, in order to make *Nada* less tender and prone to heeling, we removed a considerable amount of weight aloft by converting her from a ketch to a cutter. The existing heavy wooden masts were taken off and replaced with a single aluminum spar. I read various books on how to achieve a balanced sail plan and consulted a couple of naval architects, concluding that I needed to move the main mast back 4 feet. In order to keep the same foretriangle dimensions and headsails, I also cut down our 8-foot bowsprit by 4 feet. The project was a massive undertaking, requiring the building of a mast step inside *Nada* and moving almost all the chainplates. The hull then had to be repainted. As soon as we were done, we set sail for Cuba.

I screwed up the mast placement calculations really badly; *Nada* had the most atrocious weather helm! We had to sail with a well-reefed mainsail much of the time to partially counteract the weather helm. The mast was way too far aft, and in fact as soon as I thought about it I realized we had sailed many a time when rigged as a ketch without the mizzen sail and *Nada* had balanced beautifully—there was no reason to have moved the mast at all!

After our Cuba circumnavigation the mast was moved back to where it had been, which in turn meant moving all the chainplates once again and repainting the hull. While I was about it, I removed the reliable old hand-cranked Sabb engine and replaced it with a Yanmar, and we cut off the teak decks with an angle grinder and replaced them with a layer of fiberglass and non-skid paint; together, these measures lightened *Nada* by several hundred more pounds but even so she remained exceedingly tender, heeling to every puff of the wind.

Neither of our guidebooks has been a commercial success, but luckily my other publications have kept us going and in the meantime we have had many fascinating adventures. We took *Nada* through the Bahamas, exploring all those places we missed on our first cruise (and falling in love with the Exumas—if I only had two weeks to sail somewhere, I think this is where I would go), and up the U.S. East Coast as far as Acadia National Park in Maine (what a spectacular cruising ground this is).

As Pippin and Paul grew, *Nada* became increasingly cramped. I traded her in for a Pacific Seacraft 40, *Nada II*, with a substantial increase in interior volume and a significant improvement in upwind performance; the caprails and side decks were no longer under water. Initially, the children thought there was something wrong with the new boat and were quite disappointed!

I became heavily involved in researching hybrid and other energy and systems options for boats. For this, I needed a larger boat and the ability to add and subtract substantial battery banks, and to move engines, generators, and electric motors in and out of the boat. We traded in the Pacific Seacraft for first a Malo 45 (*Nada III*) and then a Malo 46 (*Nada IV*), essentially the same boat but with a radically different electrical system. We carried out extensive testing of cutting edge propulsion and energy systems while exploring the west coast of Sweden, much of Denmark, parts of Norway, and the north and west coasts of Scotland and Ireland together with their off-lying islands. We have had, and continue to have, many, many wonderful and memorable experiences.

I find the research and testing fascinating; Terrie finds it incredibly boring. It's been almost thirty years since our first voyage and nothing much has changed! At times we have spent weeks and months powering and sailing backward and forward in the same protected waters collecting data. I make sure we do the testing in fascinating places that provide plenty of painting opportunities for Terrie.

Meantime Paul has been bitten by the cruising bug. He has his own boat, a 1975 28-foot Cape Dory, which he restored and sailed from New Orleans to Maine and back. He and a group of equally penniless friends in New Orleans have formed the Telltales Boat Collective, and have now had another 27-foot Cape Dory donated. He has a blog at www.sailfeed.com/writers/paul-calder/.

Nada was ultimately abandoned by her new owners and left to rot in a boatyard in New York for a decade or more. And then she took on a new lease on life as the centerpiece of a non-profit organization whose mission is "to empower young people with confidence, courage and character and transform lives aboard the sailing vessel *Nada.*" The new organization (www.sailingnada. com) has lovingly restored her—she looks just as she did thirty years ago (thank you Roger and Philip). What a marvelous and fitting evolution. We were certainly young (and foolish) when we set out to build *Nada.* She gave us the experience and confidence to enjoy a wonderful life. May she now do the same for many more young people through the years.

Looking back, I can see that our 18-month West Indies exploration was little more than a shakedown cruise; we learned many lessons, and made a number of changes. We laid the foundations for a lifetime of successful cruising together.

FURTHER READING

Seminal works that strongly infl uenced us (most probably long out of print!):

General Interest
K. Adlard Coles, *Heavy Weather Sailing*
Eric Hiscock, *Cruising Under Sail*
Bernard Moitessier, *The Long Way*
Wallace Ross, *Sailpower*
Hal Roth, *After 50,000 Miles*
Miles Smeeton, *Once is Enough*
Fastnet Report, 1979

Boatbuilding, Design, and Technical
Bill Belcher, *Wind Vane Self Steering*
Francis Kinney, *Skene's Elements of Yacht Design*
The Gougeon Brothers on Boat Construction
John Guzzwell, *Modern Wooden Yacht Construction*

 **SHAKEDOWN CRUISE**

Ferenc Mate, *From a Bare Hull*
Ross Norgrove, *Cruising Rigs and Rigging*

Cruising Guides
Kline, *Yachtsman's Guide to the Bahamas*
Don Street's Cruising Guides and the Imray-Iolaire charts